No Ordinary Crime

An Authentic Tale of Justice Influenced by War Hysteria

To Don Bennett
From Jim Wilson

MAX STEPHAN IN WAYNE COUNTY JAIL
DETROIT, MICHIGAN
(Reprinted with the permission of the Detroit Free Press)

No Ordinary Crime

An Authentic Tale of Justice Influenced by War Hysteria

James R. Wilson

BROADBLADE PRESS
11314 Miller Road
Swartz Creek, MI 40473

ISBN 0-9620249-3-7

Typeset and printed in the United States of America
Sans Serif, Inc., and McNaughton & Gunn

To Florence and Ryley Wilson,
My mother and father.

The 1942 treason case in which Max Stephan, a Detroit restaurant owner, aided Peter Krug, a German escapee from a Canadian prisoner-of-war camp.

The Constitution of the United States,
Article III, Section 3;

"Treason against the United States shall consist only in levying War against them or in adhering to their Enemies, giving them Aid and Comfort. No person shall be convicted of Treason unless on the Testimony of two Witnesses to the same overt Act, or on Confession in open Court."

Contents

Illustrations

Acknowledgements

I owe a debt of gratitude to many people who willingly spent time, either in correspondence or in person, to answer my questions.

They included:

> The U. S. Bureau of Prisons personnel; Mr. J. C. Everett at Milan, Michigan; Mr. J. D. Henderson, Warden, Atlanta; Dr. Pasquale Ciccone, Director, Springfield Medical Center; and Mr. Norman Carlson, Director of Prisons, Washington.
>
> Mr. Joseph L. Kelsch of the U. S. Post Office in Detroit.
>
> Mr. Hamilton of the People's State Bank of Leslie, Michigan.
>
> The British Embassy personnel in Washington, particulary Mr. G. Owlett and Flt.Lt. P. C. Butt. The latter was most helpful in dealing with persons totally unkown to me in the Ministry of Defence in London.
>
> Mr. Nicholas Salowich, Sr. The insights and impressions he provided were most valuable. Also, my thanks go to his son, Nicholas Jr., who provided additional information.

Mr. John Bugas, former head of the Detroit FBI Office and also former Ford Motor Co. Vice President. Although he declined to grant me an interview because at that time I did not yet have access to the FBI files, his was a most informative refusal. From our brief phone conversation he told his recollections of the time when he talked to Peter Krug in Canada.

Dr. and Mrs. Vollmer, Eckehart J. Priebe, and Ulrich Steinhilper.

Mr. William Boettcher of Flint who served as my translator.

My special thanks go to Mr. Peter Krug who provided information and answered my many questions. This was all done by mail between the U.S. and Germany. Despite Mr. Krug's role in telling his story, I still must accept responsibility for the accuracy.

Preface

The early months of 1942 were, without a doubt, among the darkest days in American history. Since December 8th of 1941, the day after the Japanese attacked Pearl Harbor, we had been at war. It was a war that we were losing and it looked as though the very survival of the United States was at stake.

In those dark days, in Detroit, a German-American restaurant owner named Max Stephan committed treason against his adopted country and in so doing, became one of only a handful of convicted traitors in American history. His specific crime was that of aiding an escaped prisoner of war, a certain Peter Krug, an arrogant young product of Hitler's Germany. Krug had been a German bomber pilot until his capture and imprisonment in the Canadian POW camp from which he had escaped.

Max Stephan was not an intelligent man and his actions in helping Krug were both amateurish and stupid. The Federal prosecutors were given a classic case on the proverbial silver platter.

It is the rarity of treason cases that made Stephan's crime notable. This book, then, is the chronicle of that crime and the people involved; the good, the bad, and the indifferent.

The essence of the story is that in the darkest hours of the war, Max Stephan committed the ultimate sin. In the words of the U.S. Constitution, complete with the capitalized nouns of an older form of English, he was convicted of being a traitor to the U.S. by "adhering to their Enemies, giving them Aid and Comfort."

In 1942, at the time of Max Stephan's crime, I was 13 years old and lived in Detroit. It was my fate to see World War II from the newspapers and hear about it on the radio. I could only stare in awe at the older boys who had been "lucky" enough to be a part of it. I would see them at school and at church when they came back for a visit after basic training. I knew that I was missing the greatest experience that could ever befall me. I desperately wanted to be in the service.

I was not some isolated loony, nor was I a patriotic zealot. Actually I was quite normal and my attitude was typical. It was an era of strong patriotism, brought on primarily by the Japanese attack on Pearl Harbor. It was a war of survival, we were losing, and I knew I was needed.

I was, of course, an impressionable young boy at the time. I did not really understand the chaos and horror of war. To me it was uniforms with bright colored insignias, guns, tanks, and airplanes. The war that was in progress, we now know, was mankind's greatest conflict. A true global war.

The Russians may have had the right idea when they gave the war a name. They didn't come up with anything as lacking in creativity as "World War II." For them it was "The Great Patriotic War." I agree with them, although the name is a little too dramatic for undemonstrative Americans. The Russian name, nevertheless, described the American attitude accurately. Patriotism was preached and practiced continuously in our daily lives. It was a time of unification and common purpose. There had been a strong isolationist movement in the U.S. and it disappeared in one day, Dec. 7, 1941, when the Japanese bombed Pearl Harbor.

The war ended before I was old enough to be a part of it and to this day it bothers me. I missed the great crusade. I would never be a part of the fraternity of men who would sit around sipping beer in dark veterans' clubs, talking about Iwo, the Black Forest, Coral Sea, and a thousand other places that I had only read about and traced on a wall map.

I became part of a totally unrecognized generation. We

were the ones that left high school at the time when the veterans were returning. As was only right, they got the slots in the overcrowded colleges, they got the jobs, and naturally, the girls. My generation could have been a collective patient on the psychiatrist's couch, what with identity crises, guilt, inferiority complexes, and low self-esteem. I still wonder; should I have run away from home, lied about my age, and joined the Marines?

Actually, in 1951 I got my chance to be a part of the Korean War, and, being somewhat older, I didn't mind one bit when, quite by accident I received a rather easy stateside assignment. I was wiser and the patriotic zeal was not as rampant in the land at the time of that conflict.

This is not some idle digression, nor am I simply exercising an imaginary right to fill a Preface with self-serving remarks. Rather, it is important that we all go back in time and view the events of the story in their proper context, not according to modern standards.

The story of Max Stephan stayed with me for a long time. In the absence of more direct involvement, it had to serve as my own personal World War II story. So, one day, some 30 years after I had delivered newspapers in northwest Detroit, that told of this and a thousand other wartime events, I decided to begin to research the case. I found that my memory was faulty, but the research also uncovered many new facts, of which I had never been aware. I spent 15 years, on and off, collecting information. Once, for 8 years, I never touched the manuscript.

The facts for this book were collected from the best sources that I could find, including interviews, letters, original research, books, and files. The trial transcript and the FBI files were certainly of major importance. A complete list of sources is included in the Acknowledgements and Bibliography. Naturally, I must take responsibility for any omissions.

Chapter 1

Detroit, Saturday, April 18, 1942

It was four and a half months now, since the Japanese had bombed Pearl Harbor and brought the United States into World War II.

Almost every facet of American life was taking on some new form and appearance. Voids were being created in families as husbands and sons left home to enter the armed forces. Sweeping social change was in progress, resulting from a great migration, as people moved from the rural South to the industrial North. In Detroit, the factories were in full operation producing strange new products required in a global war. The normal peacetime products, automobiles in Detroit's case, were no longer being manufactured. People would have to make the old car last, but the job would be made easier by gas rationing and a nationwide, 40 mile per hour speed limit.

On the southeast side of Detroit, in the area around East Jefferson Avenue, the routine was now well established. The factories were operating around the clock and a walk past any one of them was like a preview of a miniature Hell. All that was visible from the street were the blinding flashes of the welders' torches as metal was attached to metal; armor to form a tank turret, or feet to the legs of a machine gun tripod. But mainly there was noise, probably no different than the factory noise of today, but it seemed more urgent.

At daybreak on April 18, 1942 the streets began to show signs of life as the merchants unlocked their doors. Awnings were being cranked down, and vegetable displays were being freshened. The sounds of the trolley cars could be heard with more frequency now. These were great, yellow monsters that swayed down the main streets, such as Jefferson, Woodward, Grand River and Michigan, trailing sparks in the dim light of early morning. They were not the delicate tourist trolleys of today, that run for a few blocks. These were utilitarian vehicles that people used for getting across town to work. They were big and they were noisy.

On that then-ordinary Saturday morning a less than ordinary event was unfolding. At daybreak a forever anonymous resident of southeast Detroit, in the East Jefferson area, opened his door and found a young man sleeping in the protection of the entrance. He swore and lashed out with a kick at the young vagrant, who quickly ran to the sidewalk and straightened his clothes.[10*]

He was dressed in workman's coveralls, unusual street wear, and a close look at his feet would have revealed that one of his shoes was an inch longer than the other, with a hole worn through the sole. One could tell that he was tired, he had slept as best he could for the past few days, but it had not been easy. Not so obvious was the fact that he had eaten very little in the last day or two. It happened to be his 22nd birthday on that very Saturday, but because of his circumstances, he looked older. He was unquestionably a handsome man and his bearing was decidedly military. He was a man who could easily have been confronted by a motherly lady on the trolley car, with the now common question, "Young man, why aren't you in the service?"

He carried identity papers that showed him to be Jean Etté, formerly a carpenter on the French liner, Normandie. That ship, once a luxurious passenger liner rivaling any in the world, was then lying on its side in its slip in New York Harbor, a gutted derelict, and an attraction for the curious. It had been swept by a catastrophic fire a month earlier.

When the young man had mixed with the pedestrian traffic,

10*Sources will be indicated with number that coincides with number in Bibliography.

he stopped and counted out three cents for a Detroit Free Press. Of all the news that day, he was concerned only with a small article on the third page.

That finished, he had much to do. He had a long journey to complete and little money or resources. He would need help and he did have the names of several people in Detroit who might provide it. It was his only hope and he had no choice but to try. Though he spoke with an accent, his English was fair enough and he proceeded in his search, which centered in the southeast corner of Detroit.

Around 8:00 A.M. he was down to the last name and address on his mental list. It was at 259 Philip Street. After making cautious inquiries, he was directed eastward on Jefferson. At about 8:45 he found the street and then had the much easier task of finding house number 259. He headed south on Philip Street, under the elm trees, and walked three blocks before finally arriving in front of the place. The neighborhood consisted of one, two, and four family houses and number 259 turned out to be a two family house with an upstairs and downstairs flat.

He approached the front door and was relieved to see that the upstairs tenant's name was "Bertelmann", the name he sought. It was Mrs. Bertelmann's name and address that he had remembered. Now he must find out if she would help him. He rang the bell and it was heard by Mrs. Bertelmann, who happened to be home alone at the time. Her upstairs button, the one that opened the downstairs door, was broken and she knew that she must descend the stairs to see who was there and let him in.

She went down to the front door and saw the young, tired stranger standing there. In English he asked if she was Mrs. Bertelmann and she replied that she was. Then he asked if she had any carpentry work, painting, or cleaning up to be done. She said she did not. Then pleading thirst, the stranger asked for a glass of water. She allowed him to come upstairs to the kitchen. He accepted the water and then revealed his true identity to her. Using his native German for the first time, he formally introduced himself. He was in fact, Lieutenant Peter

Krug, former German bomber pilot, and escapee from the Bowmanville prisoner of war camp in Ontario, Canada.

Mrs. Bertelmann almost fainted. When she regained her composure in the ensuing minutes she did the only thing she could think of, she phoned a friend, Max Stephan. In doing so she drastically altered the course of her own life and launched Max Stephan on a course that would take him to a U.S. District Court.

It was on the following Tuesday, April 21, 1942, that Detroit and the rest of America found out what had happened on the previous weekend. During that time, Max Stephan escorted Peter Krug on a grand tour of Detroit before finally putting him on a bus for Chicago. Peter Krug was still at large and Stephan was in the Wayne County Jail. Others were implicated and as the story unfolded it began to take on the appearance of a Teutonic opera, complete with a young Siegfried. Detroit would have a front row seat and would be able to cheer for the heroes and hiss at the villains, of which there were many.

The case provided a broad education. People were even motivated to dust off their copies of the U.S. Constitution. One learned that insofar as ordinary citizens were concerned, treason was the only crime specifically proscribed in the Constitution. It could be found in Article III, Section 3, and had been placed in the Constitution for a very specific reason, so the story was told. Under old English custom, at the time of our country's founding, treason had been almost anything that the King wanted it to be. It could include insulting him, holding an opinion different than his, or, perhaps unwisely, spitting in his face. Also, under those earlier customs there was only one punishment, and it was a slow, agonizing death. The drafters of the Constitution did not want any of that in their new democracy and gave treason a specific definition. Also, they were quite clear in their rules for how one could be found guilty of treason. There would be no more confessions drawn from some poor wretch, under torture. In the Constitution, it was stated that there must be two witnesses to the same overt act, or confession in open court.

We also learned about the international rules of war, particularly in respect to the treatment of prisoners. Those rules permitted a German officer in full uniform, complete with the swastika emblem of the Third Reich, to testify in a Detroit Federal Court in June of 1942. That testimony has been one of the minor mysteries of the case. Under the rules of the Geneva Convention a prisoner of war could never be forced to testify at the trial of someone who had helped him. Yet Krug, after his recapture, served voluntarily as a witness at Max Stephan's trial.

While Stephan's fate may have been sealed with or without Krug's testimony, the young enemy's appearance certainly made a landmark case even more spectacular. Detroit saw the enemy in person and Krug's manner gave them little cause for optimism about the course of the war, which was already going badly enough.

Chapter 2

A Brief History

A trip to the public library will reveal a broad spectrum of books dealing with World War II. These range from books on specific battles to the volumes written by Winston Churchill. Here, it is important to understand only the key events that led up to the world situation in April of 1942 and serve as a backdrop for this book.

In the thirties, two military dictators had risen to power in Europe; Adolph Hitler in Germany and Benito Mussolini in Italy. Hitler and Mussolini formed an alliance called the Axis, which later included Japan.

In Japan, Emperor Hirohito was the national leader, king, pope, and god, all rolled into one. No Johnny-come-lately like Hitler, his royal lineage went back for 2,000 years, to the first Emperor, Jimmu, and before that, in legend, to the sun goddess.

The Japanese had, for years, been nibbling away at the edges of China. In 1937 they invaded the central body of that country. They captured Nanking, and murdered an estimated 200,000 people there, by gun, sword, and unspeakable torture.

Adolph Hitler came to power in Germany in 1933. Germany had been in disarray since World War I and had been under restrictions in respect to rearming. In March, 1935 Hitler declared *Wehrfreiheit*, military freedom, which meant that Germany would rearm openly. No one moved to stop him. He annexed Austria in March, 1938 to the cheers of happy Austrians. Then, in October of 1938 his territorial ambitions began in earnest with the annexing of an area of Czechoslovakia called the Sudetenland. This was followed by all of Czechoslovakia in March of 1939. Again, no one moved to stop him.

Next, he signed a nonaggression pact with the Russian dictator, Joseph Stalin. That was followed by the invasion of Poland on September 1, 1939. World War II started on September 3, 1939, when Britain, France, and the British Empire which included Canada, Australia, and New Zealand, all declared war on Germany and Italy.

On September 3, the Prime Minister of Great Britain, Neville Chamberlain, appointed Winston Churchill as First Lord of the Admiralty. By the following May, Chamberlain was forced to resign and Churchill became Prime Minister.

Poland fell to Germany and Russia by the last week of September, 1939. It was a three week war. In April, 1940, Denmark and Norway surrendered to German forces. Next, Hitler invaded France and the British came to their aid. They were unable to stop the German forces however, and Paris fell in June, 1940. Whatever troops could escape the continent, escaped at Dunkirk in June, 1940 in a mass evacuation across the English Channel to England. France fell in June of 1940 and its boundaries were reduced to a fraction of what they were before, with the new capitol at Vichy.

England then stood alone against the Germans, surrounded, and with the sea routes cut off by a very effective submarine offensive.

Hitler's goal was to force Britain to come to terms. He planned to do that either by an invasion of England or by a very serious threat of invasion. In preparation for that strategy, it was necessary to gain control of the skies over the English Channel. It was then that a phase of the war called the Battle of Britain began. It was an air war, the *Luftwaffe*, the German Air Force, against the Royal Air Force, the RAF.

The Battle of Britain began in August of 1940 and ended in October. It started as a German offensive against RAF airfields and ended, or deteriorated, when the emphasis was shifted from the airfields to British cities and the civilian population.

By October it was clear that Hitler had not won superiority in the air and had abandoned his plans to invade England.

In late August, on a bombing mission that was a part of the Battle of Britain, Peter Krug's plane was shot down and he was taken prisoner by the British.

The RAF had become the heroes of the day by defeating the German air offensive. It was English history repeating itself. Much of that country's history is the story of wars with invaders from the continent. There were the Celts in the 6th century B.C. and Julius Caesar in 55 B.C. In 62 A.D., Queen Boadicea led an unsuccessful revolt against the Romans at Fort Londinium. The pilots of the RAF were an updated version of those early Britons, using planes and guns instead of swords and shields. The odds had been heavily against them, like their earlier counterparts.

Churchill immortalized them in an epic speech, when he said, "Never have so many owed so much to so few." They became "the few." Prior to his death, years later, Churchill planned his own funeral procession. Near the front was a place designated for the remaining "Few."

Hitler, having received a bloody nose in the skies over England, changed his plans. He repudiated his nonaggression pact with Stalin and invaded Russia in June, 1941. The strength of the German war machine, at that time, must not be under estimated. Even while Germany was fighting a war in Russia on a broad front that reached from Leningrad to the Crimea, it was four years after the Dunkirk evacuation before the Allies would be able to recross the English Channel with an invasion force.

For Hitler and the German people, the invasion of Russia eventually turned in to a disastrous defeat. Hitler was later compared to the Pied Piper of Hamelin. In that folk story, the villagers had struck a deal with the piper to rid their village of rats, and he led their youth away, never to be seen again. Having come to power in 1933, Hitler's ideologies soon had permeated the school curriculums. He spoke of a "Thousand year Reich." He fell short of his goal by 988 years, but no one could have guessed that in 1938. By then, there was a generation of Germans who knew little else but Hitler's propaganda. Peter Krug was one of them.

Certainly, one must ask questions; What were Hitler's objectives? How did he rally the German people around him? There were several factors. Hitler sought *Lebensraum*, living room, for the German people. He sought to regain honor, lost in the treaty that concluded World War I. Germany's financial troubles he attributed to the Jews, who he accused of being international money manipulators, and he sought to make Germany free of them. It was also necessary, Hitler said, to be rid of the Jews so as to prevent racial pollution of the pure Germanic stock, a superior race. Six million Jews died in the extermination camps built by the Nazis.

Of all the leaders and conflicts since some nameless Neanderthal man picked up a stick and used it as an extension of his hand, there is no one person who has been responsible for more deaths than Adolph Hitler. Not Genghis Khan, Tamerlane, Attila the Hun, or anyone else. He was a charismatic leader and a brilliant speaker and his message struck a chord with most, but certainly not all, German people. Theirs was an ordered and disciplined society, and much of the killing was done under the tired excuse that went, "I was not responsible, I was only following orders."

In 1933, the same year that Hitler came to power, Franklin D. Roosevelt, became the 32nd President of the United States. His popular mandate was to effect a remedy for a brutal economic depression. He served through the depression and most of the war. Coincidentally, he died in April of 1945, the month and year of Hitler's death.

On the other side of the world from Hitler, another confrontation was looming. The Japanese were intent on dominating all of southeast Asia and the islands of the south Pacific. The U.S. was just as intent on preventing their domination.

Without warning, on December 7, 1941, the Japanese attacked the United States Pacific fleet at Pearl Harbor in the Hawaiian Islands. It was an act of stupidity, and how they didn't see that it was, is impossible to understand. Anyone even remotely familiar with the tactics of an ordinary fistfight knows that if you are a little guy and you want to beat up a big guy, you'd better get in one big, surprise punch and then run like hell. The punch was not a total success for the Japanese. Their high command remorsefully noted that the U.S. aircraft carriers were, somehow, missing from Pearl Harbor at the time of the attack. It looked like the big guy was going to get up a little sooner than expected and boy, was he going to be mad.

On Dec. 8, 1941, President Roosevelt declared war on the Axis powers; Japan, Germany, and Italy. The Pearl Harbor attack was devastating and the Japanese were provided with a strong advantage for many months to come. They invaded the Philippines and the final resistance there was by a small group of U.S. troops on the Bataan Peninsula and on the Island of Corregidor. Bataan fell on April 9, 1942 and the American troops taken prisoner by the Japanese were sent on the infamous "Death March." U.S. troops in the Philippines felt very deeply that they had been deserted by Roosevelt and the American people. Their bitterness was reflected outwardly in one of their songs;[8]

> "We're the poor battling bastards of Bataan,
> No mother, no father, and no Uncle Sam."

By April of 1942 there was little or no good news. The newspapers tried to be optimistic. A typical headline started in large letters;

ALLIES ESCAPE NAZI TRAP

then in small letters underneath;

Retreat 35 miles

In retrospect, those old headlines sound like the predecessors of our present "good news, bad news" jokes.

At the start of the war, experts had predicted that we would finish off the Japanese in 30 to 90 days. These estimates were not even being revised, they were being ignored as if they had never been said. But the Japanese were fought as much with racial slurs as with bullets. They were "little yellow japs." We were told that they all had weak eyes and couldn't shoot straight. Hatred for the Japanese spilled over onto thousands of loyal Americans, who happened to be of Japanese ancestry. They were placed in detention camps for no good reason.

It's still possible to capture some of the sentiment of that era. Watch your local TV guide and be prepared to stay up until about 2 A.M. Occasionally you will see an old 1942 or 1943 war movie listed. Hollywood cranked out many of these at the time. They could only deal with battles we were losing, so they ended with loud patriotic music and some epic words passing by on the screen. They bore no resemblance to real war. The "japs", who were probably Chinese actors, usually charged down a path in single file so that the outnumbered Americans could pick them off one at a time, until a mortar shell wounded them and they were bayoneted by a grinning "jap".

I forgot to mention, we saw those movies in black and white. Now they are "colorized" in artificial-looking greens and blues. Watch them on a black and white TV, if possible.

In spite of the bad news in early 1942, on April 18, the day when Peter Krug, posing as the Frenchman, Jean Etté, was searching for help along Jefferson Avenue in Detroit, an event was unfolding that may have been the start of the road back, at least in the war against the Japanese. The big guy was still a little groggy, but he was starting to sit up and rub his jaw. On that day, half way around the world from Detroit, 85 Americans in 16 B25 bombers were launching themselves from the carrier Hornet in the midst of a gale. Their mission, under the leadership of General James Doolittle, was to bomb mainland Japan, an act of defiance that the Japanese, in their worst nightmares, could not have imagined.

Due to the sighting of a Japanese ship that was promptly sunk, they were forced to launch from a greater distance than originally planned. By noon on the 18th they were causing destruction and panic in Tokyo, Kobe, Osaka, and Nagoya. By evening they were crashing into the sea along the China coast. Of the 85 men, 55 miraculously returned.

Chapter 3

Jailers to the Empire

In one day, in August of 1940, Peter Krug's short career as bomber pilot ended and he was a prisoner of war (POW). He became part of a special group, a group that exists only when the parties in a war subscribe to reasonably civilized rules.

Prisoners are both useful and bothersome. They are useful because they provide intelligence. Even without questioning them, much can be learned. Does a soldier have a three day growth of beard? Is there water in his canteen? How much ammunition is he carrying? The answers to those questions provide knowledge of the enemy's ability to wage war.

They are bothersome for many reasons. They must be guarded and fed. They may be difficult to handle. They can be disruptive and they actively do things to make sure that their captors expend as much manpower as possible in guarding them.

That was the situation in England at the time of the Battle of Britain in August through October of 1940. The English had collected some German land troops during the war in Europe, some naval forces from the sea battles, and then, during the Battle of Britain, England collected large numbers of air crewmen; pilots, gunners, and all the rest. Other prisoners in Britain, came from the desert war in North Africa, from Rommel's *Afrika Korps.*

Most of the supplies that England needed to wage war and sustain its civilian population, troops, and even the prisoners, came to England by ship. Hitler was conducting a very effective submarine war against those supply ships and large quantities of material had simply gone to the bottom of the Atlantic. The problem of having a large number of prisoners to feed and guard was something that needed a quick solution.

The solution was quite logical. Since supply ships were "deadheading" back to Canada, the prisoners could be sent there quite conveniently. The Canadians became the "Jailers to the Empire," a term that they coined in reference to themselves. Of course there was more to it than just shipping the prisoners to Canada. Camps would have to be built and guards would have to be furnished. But there was a potential benefit to the Canadians that would even accrue to the British. The prisoners could be put to work on farms and in non-military work and would help replace manpower that was off fighting the war. Whatever the British logic, the decision created considerable anguish for the prisoners, who would now be sent to Canada, much like London pickpockets in another age, being transported to the colonies.

The movement of the prisoners was not made without controversy, and points could be found in International law to support whatever viewpoint one held. The Geneva Convention stipulated that prisoners were not to be held in battle zones. It also stipulated that they were not to be subjected to excessive danger. The British could claim that their home island was a battle zone. Therefore, they could claim that they were justified in moving them. On the other hand, the prisoners could cite the danger from their own U-boats as representing excessive danger. Whatever the validity of the two positions, it is doubtful that the British spent much time in debate with the prisoners. The reality of the situation simply added up to a long sea excursion for the captives.[1]

Following news of impending transfer the prisoners could do little more than express their displeasure in an occasional riot. Their problem with the transfer to Canada went far beyond the bounds of the Geneva Convention and even the U-boat danger. Early in the Battle of Britain the prisoners were overflowing with arrogance as they looked forward to an early release when the invasion of England came. But even the staunchest of German optimists were aware that the rest of the Empire might never be brought to terms. Once in Canada it could be a very long time before their Austrian house painter might be able to bring them back.

Then, as the Battle of Britain drew to a close the new arrivals brought more bad news—the invasion fleet had been disbanded. It was now beginning to look like escape was the only answer. As long as they were in England it was at least possible to think about a cross channel dash in a stolen boat. From across the Atlantic it was a different matter.

For a prisoner of war, escape has always been regarded as a military duty as well as a personal aim, simply to be free. There were, in fact, many escapes from Canadian camps but only one prisoner actually succeeded in returning from Canada to Germany during the war. Peter Krug's escape may have been the closest anyone came to being the second.

The prisoners were transported to Canada in ordinary merchant ships making their return journeys. The ships would have other passengers, such as RAF trainees and members of the various free forces, the Norwegians for example, bound for training camps in Canada. Prior to departure each prisoner was given a small Red Cross card to sign. The British had taken the trouble to preprint a message on it which read in German, "I am well, I am being transferred to Canada." The prisoners, having been spared the ordeal of writing a long message, simply signed the cards and addressed them to their next of kin.[1]

The plots and intrigue, common in the camps, continued at sea. In one case a plan was developed to take over a ship. The prisoners had disguised themselves as crewmen and walked around the ship collecting information and weapons. The nearness of a British cruiser discouraged the prisoners and nothing came of it.[1]

The usual port of entry was Halifax, Nova Scotia. At first the townspeople would gather at the docks to watch them disembark. It was a popular pastime to jeer and hiss, but after a few boatloads, the sport lost its thrill. The prisoners in their ill-fitting clothes hardly looked worth the effort.[1]

At the docks the prisoners were placed on trains and immediately came under the care of their official hosts, the Veterans' Guard of Canada. This was an organization hurriedly put together when Canada became the jailers. The Guard consisted mainly of World War I veterans who were past the age for active duty in World War II. This also meant that they were older than most of their charges and would sometimes be hard pressed in physical confrontations. They served as sentries, commanders, and all the ranks between, at the camps and on the trains. They performed their duties with correctness, with only a few exceptions probably brought on by extreme frustration.

The trains carried the prisoners to the many camps that were appearing across Canada from Quebec to the Great Plains. The one prisoner who succeeded in getting back to Germany jumped from such a train. He was Franz von Werra, a fighter pilot who already had two escapes behind him in England. Von Werra was a colorful and cocky character who was sometimes given to exaggeration when describing his exploits. There is even some question about the legitimacy of his use of "von" in front of his name. His British captors once pointed out to him that somehow his name had been omitted from the *Almanach de Gotha*, the official book of titles.[1]

It was in January of 1941 that he jumped from a train that was taking him and his fellow prisoners to Camp W, above Lake Superior. Several others escaped from the train but they were recaptured. The train was filled with many of the "difficult" prisoners who would continue to figure heavily in escapes. Many of them had been captured in the Battle of Britain.

The prisoners were seated in groups of four in the open coach cars. One group of four contained both Peter Krug and von Werra. Von Werra put his plan into action when the train was near the St. Lawrence River. One prisoner held up a blanket as if to fold it. Behind that screen, two other prisoners quickly opened the window. In an instant, von Werra dove through and fortunately landed in a snow bank. The window was quickly closed behind him. It all happened faster than it can be told and his absence was not detected until later.[1]

Von Werra made his way to the St. Lawrence River, crossed the narrow, unfrozen strip of water in a stolen rowboat, and landed in Ogdensburg, New York. That being January of 1941, the U.S. was still neutral. Nevertheless, he was detained by the police and held a short time. His release was initiated by the German Consulate in New York City that paid von Werra's $50,000 bond. He was the only prisoner freed in that manner. From then on, all were returned to Canada. Once free on bail von Werra paused long enough to make the rounds of New York café society, and then fled to Mexico. From there he went to South America where he caught the last Italian commercial flight to Italy. The Germans considered the $50,000 bail as money well spent and gladly forfeited it. He was back in Germany in April, 1941 and was a valuable source of information about such things as British intelligence methods. The British even felt that they could detect the diminished intelligence value of "post von Werra" prisoners. He was awarded a decoration, of course, and was married in a much publicized ceremony. Six months later he was dead. After rejoining the *Luftwaffe*, his Messerschmidt malfunctioned and he crashed into the English Channel. It was a testimony to the accelerated actuarial tables that govern all fighter pilots.[1]

Camp W, the camp he never reached, was reputed to be one of the worst camps in Canada. Its location above Lake Superior is an area of bitterly harsh winters and the conditions in the camp provoked at least one hunger strike. One might wonder what a group of German prisoners could accomplish with a hunger strike. It was calculated to draw the attention of the Swiss authorities who inspected camps on both sides and verified compliance with the Geneva Convention.

At the other end of the spectrum were camps such as the one at Grand Ligne in Quebec. There, General von Ravenstein, Canada's highest ranking prisoner, languished in relative comfort. He had been captured in North Africa. It cannot be verified with absolute certainty, but one prisoner may have been more notable. That was Harald Quandt who was the son by a previous marriage of Magda Goebbels. She was the wife of Joseph Goebbels, Propaganda Minister of the Third Reich.

The Monteith Camp held 4,000 enlisted men, including a complete band that was captured intact with all their instruments, by General Montgomery's troops on D-day. Monteith was also said to be the temporary home of Paratrooper Brosik who had escaped more times than anyone else.[2]

Hardly a week went by that the Canadians did not uncover some new and creative escape plot. Tunneling was common although the fliers did not, in general, like them. Most tunnels were reinforced with wood, which was usually taken from the buildings that the prisoners lived in. Tin cans from the kitchen, with both their tops and bottoms cut off, could be used to form an air duct. In at least one tunnel, camp electricity was used to power an air pump.

Of all the camps, Bowmanville, near Toronto was undoubtedly the most outstanding. Many of the Camp W prisoners were later moved there and had to admit that conditions were *nicht schlecht*—not bad. Before the war, Bowmanville had been a boys' reformatory and when it was a prisoner of war camp the sign still read "Bowmanville Boys Reformatory." Canadian papers were frequently critical of its "posh" conditions. Due to its former role it contained a gymnasium, a swimming pool, and other features such as a fine stainless steel kitchen. Newspaper criticism was aimed at those things and others, the truckloads of beer, for example, sometimes seen being shipped in. The prisoners were allowed a beer ration. All camps had a canteen where such refreshment was available. Tokens were issued for the beer. It was rumored that an officer received two new uniforms each year. Bowmanville was an officers' camp so there was a company of enlisted prisoners held there solely to perform the more menial duties not generally expected of an officer in any army.

If one wonders at the reason, or even the need, for this treatment, it should be remembered that the Germans held a great number of Allied prisoners. It was important that nothing be done to cause retaliation on those unfortunates, whose lot, at best, was worse than anything endured by the Germans in Canada.

At its height, Bowmanville held 800 prisoners although at

the time of Krug's escape it held 500. The Canadian Commandant, Lt.Col. R.O. Bull, was generally respected by the prisoners as a fair man.

Eventually there were two German Generals captured in North Africa that were held there, one was von Ravenstein who was moved from the Grand Ligne camp. They kept to themselves and had little to do with the other prisoners. Also held there was one of Germany's heroes, Otto Kretschmar, a former U-boat captain. He had been one of Germany's top three U-boat aces. All three were lost to Germany at about the same time. The other two had been less fortunate, they had gone down with their ships.

Military discipline and rank continued to be the system of government in the camps. The senior prisoners were in charge and those of lower rank were expected to follow orders. A soldier that defied a military order in a POW camp could expect the same punishment that he would get if not a prisoner. It may be after the war, but the punishment would come. Through the military structure, they organized activities such as classes in English. International law as it applied to prisoners was taught so that they all could become jailhouse lawyers. Navigation classes were conducted for naval personnel. In officers' camps such as Bowmanville, sports were organized. Hockey, a popular game in both Canada and Germany, became a winter pastime. In fact, Reinhardt Pfundtner, a German hockey star, was held at Bowmanville. Enlisted men in other camps were spared from the problems of idleness and the accompanying muscle atrophy. They were, quite legally, put to work on farms. That was really a blessing. Their work gave many of them a large measure of freedom. The fortunate ones were able to move about in a surprisingly normal manner as they became more trusted.[7]

The Germans had a more sinister problem, however, and that was the presence of hard core Nazis among them.[7] There were cases of kangaroo courts and murders by those groups of fanatics, who served as ideological prosecutors. The number of prisoners who were killed in escape attempts is about equal to the number murdered by Nazi fanatics.

Escape was the overriding obsession of many. Otto Kretschmar planned a mass escape from Bowmanville in which he and others were to be met at the coast by U-boats. It was an elaborate tunnel plan and it failed due to a massive cave-in caused when another prisoner, apparently not in on the plan, dug some topsoil for his garden. Kretschmar never tried again. It was said that he became involved in intelligence gathering. His sources of information were the newspapers and magazines that might be left by guards. Anything worthwhile was sent back to Germany in coded letters to relatives who had been told to turn over all letters to German intelligence.[2]

Other plots were conducted by two man teams or solo. One notable loner at Bowmanville was Ulrich Steinhilper whose preference, at first, was to simply carry some small sticks. When the guards were not looking he would prop up the wire with the sticks and slip out.[10]

As escapes began to occur with more regularity, the Canadians were able to make a simple observation. It was generally the same ones who escaped or were involved in the plots. Therefore, a special escape proof camp was built at Gravenhurst Barracks, an Army camp 75 miles north of Bowmanville. It became the home of the "top escapers", the *Ausbrecher Könige von Kanada* (The Escape Kings of Canada), as they were called years later in a German book by that name. A Canadian Staff Sergeant named McGurn even immortalized himself in Germanic literature when he told the prisoners, who were going to Gravenhurst, that the camp had the "most beautiful fence in Canada." It was said that his false teeth flashed as he described the finger thick wire, set in concrete.[10]

One prisoner, Walter Manhart, made a special wire cutter and escaped through the Gravenhurst fence. He made a clean getaway but it was late in the war and the borders of the Third Reich were so diminished that it would have been impossible for him to return. He took a new identity, becoming a tennis instructor on Long Island, New York. It was not until 1957 that he returned to Germany.

Motivation for escape varied among individuals. For some it was the challenge, for some the overwhelming desire to be free, and for some it was simple loyalty to the German cause. Many felt that as long as they were physically able they must do what they could. Some had specific missions, a message to carry back.

The escapes were not frolicsome adventures. As with the Allied prisoners, these were young men spending five and six years at the prime of their lives behind barbed wire. Peter Krug was captured in 1940 at the age of 20 and except for a few weeks during escapes, was confined until 1946 when he was 26. A prisoner could be wounded or killed in the attempt and in fact some were. They all knew the risk when they went near the wire. Inside the better camps like Bowmanville, life could be reasonably comfortable, still recognizing the absence of certain amenities—the company of women for one. There were Hollywood movies complete with gangsters, there was sports, beer, study, reading and the like. Given the risk of escaping and the chances of crossing the Atlantic, many simply settled into prison routine.

The physical experience of being outside the camp, a fugitive in a strange land, was exhausting. It was necessary to have a reasonably good knowledge of English and even the best had a typically German accent. One escapee's pronunciation of Carthage (New York) caused his recapture.[10] Sleep was difficult and the slightest mistake could cause suspicion and arrest. It was a nerve wracking existence and most were caught under the most chance circumstances imaginable. Money was another problem. It was difficult to obtain until later in the war and earlier escapes were made with little or no money.

There was no real underground railway to help them. Contacts could be made but for the most part the escapee had to survive on his wits.

As the prisoners first began to arrive in Canada in late 1940 and early 1941 they learned that they did indeed have some friends nearby. The U.S. was not yet in the war and communication channels between Germany and the U.S. were open and operating. German-Americans were encouraged to send relief packages to the prisoners in Canada and the activity could be performed quite openly and legally, even after Dec. 7, 1941 when the U.S. declared war on the Axis powers.

In many cities small groups were formed under various names, for example, "The Red Cross Ladies" or "The Chicago Knitting Club."[7] They might meet weekly to prepare packages of knitted socks, mittens for Camp W, sweaters, food, and tobacco. The articles might be collected from friends, handmade, or purchased. However the packages had a second, and more sinister, purpose. Hidden inside would sometimes be special inks, special paper, and bookbinding material. Those supplies could be, and in fact were, used by the prisoners to forge passports, U.S. Selective Service cards, and other special identification for use in escapes. It was strongly rumored, later, that the lists of the prisoners' needs in that regard, came straight from Berlin. If that was true, Berlin probably got the information from the coded letters sent by the prisoners to their relatives.

In any event, it was required that the packages carry a return address. Sometimes the donors concealed their names and addresses in the package in some way. The addresses were carefully saved by the prisoners and as the collection at Bowmanville grew, it became obvious that there were centers of German sentiment. At least three cities stood out; Chicago, Detroit, and Buffalo. In the absence of a formal underground railway, the addresses in, and on, the packages would have to do.

Lieutenant Peter Krug, having been moved from Camp W to Bowmanville, and still with visions of von Werra literally disappearing into freedom before his very eyes, noticed a particularly heavy flow of packages from Detroit, just across the river from Windsor, Ontario. One address in particular was:

Mrs. Margareta Bertelmann
259 Philip St.
Detroit, Michigan
USA

Chapter 4

Max Stephan

Most average, middle-class Americans, at the time of World War II would not care to have known Max Stephan. He was a backslapper, a teller of crude jokes, and in general, an overweight loudmouth. Worse yet, he was ardently pro-German.

In no way could he be regarded as a typical German-American in the World War II era. Most German-Americans were simply ordinary Americans who served their country with little thought of their origins. The blue and the gold stars appeared in their windows, just like everyone else's. Max Stephan was, however, typical of a small pro-German and pro-Nazi lunatic fringe that was active in the U.S. in the late thirties and early forties. There could have been two dozen different German societies active in the U.S. at the time. However, their focal point and most widely known organization was the German-American Bund, known to the general public because of its well-publicized, evangelical like rallies of enormous size. Its most notable one was held in New York in December of 1941. Behind the podium was a giant picture of Adolph Hitler, flanked by smaller pictures of Washington and Lincoln.

While Stephan denied being a member of the Bund, he was well acquainted with Bund members, and when he eventually had a restaurant, it was a popular Bund meeting place.

Stephan was born in Cologne, Germany in 1892. As long as he was in Germany, his life centered in that city. Cologne was a center for German culture, history, and industry. Little of the culture part apparently ever rubbed off on Max Stephan, however. At the age of six he was enrolled in public school and continued his formal education for eight years, until he was fourteen. For a potential lifetime member of the great working class, that was a standard education in Germany at the time. Having completed it, he went to work as a grocer's apprentice, still in Cologne, and followed that vocation for about six years.

In 1912, when he was 19 years old, he entered the German army for what he thought would be his two years of compulsory military service. Before that obligation was completed, however, World War I broke out. Having gotten an early start, a leg up, so to speak, he was already a lance corporal when the war started. By 1915 he was a sergeant. It was not bad for a grocer's apprentice. He saw action with a unit from Alsace-Lorraine, it may have been the 99th German Infantry, and Stephan claimed to have been in important battles of World War I. He always added, quickly, that he never fought against the Americans, only the French.

He claimed that of the 120 men in his company at the start of the war, only he and five others were left at the end. Two fingers of his left hand were permanently crippled from bullet wounds received at Rheims. Because of his injuries he was reassigned to noncombatant duties in 1915. At first that consisted of serving as a guard at a prison for German soldiers convicted of such crimes as deserting their units. In 1917 and 1918 he served as a censor in a military post office. His job was to read soldiers' letters and clip away military secrets and discouraging news.

In 1918, with six years of service behind him, Stephan left the army. His wounds were apparently not seriously debilitating because he was able to take a job with the German National Police, serving in Cologne. Undoubtedly his military police duties, when he was a guard at the prison, served him well in getting the civilian police job.

On October 30, 1922 he married Agnes Junger, also of Cologne. In 1924 he had served in the National Police for six years. He could add that to his military service and claim a

AGNES (JUNGER) STEPHAN
(Reprinted with the permission of the Detroit Free Press)

total of twelve years national service. That was a magic number, making him eligible for one of two options. He could accept a guaranteed lifetime job in the national service or he could take a discharge with a bonus of 9,000 marks. He took the golden handshake and at the age of 31 opened a *bierstube* or saloon in Cologne. During his *bierstube* days he learned English.

In 1928, four years after buying the *bierstube*, he sold it and prepared to emigrate to Canada. He blamed high taxes, inflation, and bad business conditions. The political climate was changing but Stephan never made any reference to that when questioned about it in later years. It may not have been a factor but by then the SA, the *Sturmabteilung*, was in the streets shouting "*Deutschland erwache*"—Germany awake.

Stephan arrived alone in the city of Quebec on October 20, 1928. Agnes would follow later. He had $3,000 in his pocket, almost a small fortune at that time. He went directly to Windsor, Ontario, across the Detroit River from the city of Detroit. On December 28 Stephan found employment with General Motors of Canada as a repairman. In his application he listed the Smith Motor Company of Milwaukee as his previous employer, having worked there four years, he claimed. He also claimed four dependents. By themselves the lies could have been completely harmless. Probably a high percentage of applications contained such creative embellishment, set down by people who only wanted a start. Once hired, they could demonstrate their ability, and no one would ever care what the application said. In the case of Stephan, however, his lies would come back to haunt him.

In January of 1929 Agnes joined Max in Windsor. She began to learn English at that time but never became as fluent in it as Max. In the next several months the couple prepared for the day when they could get back to doing what Max apparently liked best; running a sleazy bar. With Prohibition in the U.S., across the river, there was certainly an opportunity to make money at it in Windsor.

On July 3, 1929, Max quit his job at General Motors and he and Agnes opened a restaurant. Although they did not possess a liquor license it was generally known that a customer, if properly introduced, would not go thirsty at Max Stephan's. It was also said that an unmarried couple, unmarried to each other, that is, could get a room with a bed.

In 1929, soon after opening the restaurant, an event occurred that was to pose a mystery, in the much later episode with Peter Krug and throw additional suspicion on the Stephans.

An American couple, the Sangers from Detroit, were building a summer home on the Canadian side of the river. The location was upriver from Windsor, across from Peche Isle. Each weekend the Sangers would drive across from Detroit and check the progress on the home. They formed a habit of stopping at the Stephan's restaurant and the two couples became good friends. One thing about Max Stephan seemed to be that if he wanted to be your friend, he probably wanted something from you. At least that was the case in 1929 when Max befriended the Sangers. The Stephans wanted to become American citizens and in 1929, as now, that required five years residency. The wheels were turning in Max's head. If he could establish residency in the U.S. but stay in Windsor and run the restaurant, which was a good source of income, he would have the best of both worlds. The Sangers, at some risk to themselves, agreed to provide the needed help. A deal was struck and for residency purposes the Stephans would use the Sangers' Detroit address. That meant all mail relative to citizenship would be mailed to the Sangers who would have to personally deliver it to the Stephans. While there was no proof, no doubt the Sangers were rewarded for this service in some way other than just having Max for a friend; maybe free drinks or a meal occasionally.

When the falsification was uncovered in 1942, Mr. Sanger was dead and his wife could not remember ever having handled any mail for the Stephans. Many of the fringe participants in the case had similar lapses of memory. She also stated that she never dreamed that the restaurant she and her husband had visited, thirteen years earlier, was "that kind of place."

In 1942 the boathouse at the Sangers' place was part of an

STEPHAN'S RESTAURANT

Stephan's Restaurant on East Jefferson near the foot of Belle Isle Bridge. The building was deep and had a meeting room in the back for 150 people. This photo is from FBI files taken after the business was closed. Note fresh paint covering the word "German" in the gable end.

alternate, but unfounded theory, in respect to how Peter Krug had crossed the Detroit River.

On September 4, 1929 the Stephans rode the ferry across the

river to Detroit and applied for U.S. visas, using the false address. They then took the ferry back, probably chuckling at how they had outsmarted the *dummkopf Amerikaners*, and resumed their life in Windsor—it was business as usual.

Later they quit the first restaurant and opened a new one, still in Windsor. There were frequent liquor violations at the new location and on at least one occasion unmarried couples were caught in beds on an upstairs floor. Maybe a new morality, if there is such a thing, takes some of the impact out of that, but it was scandalous enough at the time. Prohibition was still the law in the U.S. and the tavern business in Windsor continued to be good. Stephan could probably afford to pay the occasional $100 and $200 fines that put him in the Windsor police records.

On December 2, 1931 Agnes went to the U.S. and made an application to visit Germany. Naturally, she used the Detroit address. The trip was made on June 7, 1932. She returned to the U.S. and then to Windsor on August 28, 1932. Then, still in 1932, they moved to Riverside Drive in Windsor and the city directory listed Max as a salesman for the Walkerville Brewing Company.

In 1933 it was clear that Prohibition was drawing to a close in the U.S. The "noble experiment" had failed. That was good news to anyone who was contemplating American citizenship and whose chosen profession was that of bar owner. Max fit that profile and in that year the couple moved across the river and began living in Detroit. For the first six months they rented an apartment on West Grand Boulevard. Then they found what was to become the "German Restaurant" at 7209 East Jefferson. They moved from West Grand Boulevard to the living quarters over the restaurant and one could say that things were falling into place for the 41 year old former grocer's apprentice. On May 1, 1934 it was again legal to sell liquor in Michigan, but Max had one small problem; he was an alien and could not qualify for a liquor license. For Max, that was only a minor challenge and he obtained a license in someone else's name. He operated on that license for a year and a half until he could obtain one in his own name.

On June 24, 1935 Max and Agnes Stephan proudly gave their pledge to the U.S. and renounced allegiance to all foreign kings, powers, and potentates. They were then U.S. citizens, although fraudulent ones, having falsified the residency requirement.

The "German Restaurant" gradually became a hub of German activity. On the walls were German scenes, world maps, and pictures of Hamburg Line ships. The restaurant's size was deceiving when viewed from the street. In the back was a large dining room with capacity for 150 people. Further in the back was a small rifle and pistol range suitable for .22 caliber ammunition. This was known only to a few and was found later when the FBI searched the building.

The restaurant was a popular place to go, even for non-Germans who enjoyed the kitschy atmosphere and the back-slapping, story telling owner. With a little luck one might be treated to one of Max's jokes; "Why is a German like a flea? Because he will never turn his back on you." Or, if that's not bad enough; "Why is a German like a fly? Because he's in everybody's business but his own." Max had these printed on small cards and readily gave them out. Presumably they were not copyrighted.

The restaurant was renowned for its fine German beer, even by the FBI.

The back room was available for weddings, parties, and club meetings. Stephan usually did not charge for its use, but of course, all food and drink would be purchased from him. The back room became a popular meeting place for a number of German organizations such as the Schwaben Society, a regional group, the Steuben Society, and the more sinister Kyffhaueser Bund—an outgrowth of *Stahlhelm* (Steelhelmet), a militant World War I German veterans' group. The Kyffhaueser Bund was registered with the State of Michigan and its papers listed Stephan's restaurant as its meeting place.

The regular German-American Bund also met at Stephan's although he claimed to have told them, "No uniforms, no swastikas, and no heils." Stephan claimed membership only in the Steuben Society.

In August of 1939 Stephan's reputation began to become a matter of public knowledge.

Europe was literally poised on the brink of war. In Washington the so-called Dies Committee on un-American activities was busy with its investigation of the Bund. Fritz Kuhn, the leader of the Bund in America, was in the midst of his testimony. The revelations in Washington were sufficient to prod a Detroit Free Press reporter to do what any good reporter would do; find a local connection. A local Bund meeting would be ideal, of course, and a little checking disclosed that one was scheduled to be held at Stephan's restaurant on Friday night, August 18, 1939.

When the reporter's story was run, it was alongside the continuing Washington Bund story.

On that Friday night, 75 people, probably including one or two FBI agents, met in Stephan's back dining room. Two speakers were scheduled. The first was a certain Calvin Furlong whose claim of being part Indian, English, and Irish would have placed him only a notch or two above the gypsies on Hitler's racial scale. Furlong claimed to have investigated the Bund and found it to be 100% for the American government. He criticized the New Deal initially but as the theme of his speech unfolded it was apparent that Calvin Furlong was little more than an itinerant Jew baiter.

Furlong was followed by John H. Schreiber, local Bund leader. He was six feet tall, wore his hair in a crew cut and spoke with a crisp German accent, so it was said. He only spoke briefly and closed the meeting with the words, "Free America." Later, asked for an explanation, he said that it meant, "Free America from international influence." Since the Bund itself was a form of international influence, a more explicit answer was clearly necessary. Furlong was ready to help explain. He said it really meant, "Free America of the Jews."

There was nothing comical about the meeting or the people. This was not a simple ethnic group keeping up their ties with the old country. These were furtive individuals and one of their major objectives was to nurture anti-Semitism. Given the opportunity, and possibly a few more members, they would have been conducting their own *Kristalnacht* (Crystal night, the smashing of Jewish store windows) right there in Detroit.

At another Bund Meeting, the speaker was an employee of the Wayne County prosecutor's office.

On September 1, 1939, two weeks after the meeting that was reported in the Free Press, war came once again to Europe. Max's restaurant would not be news again for two years and eight months. But that did not mean that nothing was happening there.

Before the U.S. entry into the war, when Canada began collecting the large numbers of German prisoners, Stephan let the so-called Red Cross Ladies meet at the restaurant. They would gather there to knit and otherwise prepare their packages for Canada. Stephan sold them tobacco and cigars at wholesale, to include in the parcels. The group sent fifty pounds of sausage per month to the prisoners which possibly was enjoyed along with the beer allotment.

One of the ladies in the group was Mrs. Margareta Bertelmann, originally from the Munchen-Gladbach section of Germany. Part of her and her husband Richard's background was similar to that of the Stephans. The Bertelmanns had been married in 1920. They had come to Windsor in 1928 and to the U.S. in 1929. Mr. Bertelmann had become a citizen in 1935. Mrs. Bertelmann, however, was still an alien. She was to claim that she thought she was a citizen by virtue of her husband's citizenship. She was mistaken. Her husband's citizenship would only have made it possible for her to become a citizen more quickly. It turned out to be a fortunate misunderstanding for her.

In 1942 Mr. Bertelmann was a $130 a week supervisor in a tool factory. From all indications he was a solid citizen, quite unlike Stephan. The Bertelmanns and their 20 year old daughter, Ingeborg, lived in the upstairs flat at the address on Philip Street, known even at Bowmanville.

A much more sinister character, and one who would figure prominently in the episode with Peter Krug, was a friend of Max's by the name of Theodore Donay. He was born Thaddeus

Marian Adalbert Donaj in Posen, Poland. It is difficult to say if, from an ethnic standpoint, Donay was German or Polish but it is not difficult to say what Donay considered himself to be. He regarded himself to be a Prussian and acted the part almost to comic exaggeration. Posen was indeed the name of his birthplace when he was born, prior to the first World War. The Polish name for the city is Poznan, just like Gdansk, where the Solidarity movement is so active, was formerly Danzig. Poland's boundaries had undergone severe change in the 200 years prior to World War I. From 1793 to 1919, Posen, or Poznan, on the Warta River, was in a section that had been annexed by Prussia. Therefore, Donay could rightfully claim to be a Prussian by birth.

Donay moved with his family to Berlin when he was a young boy. Later when he was arrested in connection with Stephan, the papers called him a relic of German medievalism. The comment was made partly in reference to his dueling scars, received at Altenburg University. There was someone in Detroit at the time who had been at Altenburg University as a freshman when Donay was a senior. That person said that Donay had indeed belonged to the "Ernestinia" dueling society. That anonymous person said that Donay's dueling record was not quite as glorious as he would have people believe. On one occasion, so the story went, one of Donay's duels had to be stopped because his opponent, a much older man, had a heart attack.

Donay, like the Stephans and Richard Bertelmann, had been naturalized in 1935. In the first World War Donay had been a corporal in the German Army. After the war he became an engineer for the Ford Motor Company in their German factory. In 1928 he was sent to Windsor to study production methods for the new Model A Ford, the replacement for the tired Model T. Later he went to Detroit and obtained a job in an auto plant. Later still, he opened his own business, the German-American Import Company at 3152 Gratiot in Detroit. He imported patent medicines and novelties from Germany and had visited there in 1936 and 1938. Like another ex-corporal, Adolph Hitler, he neither smoked nor drank. In

EUROPE IMPORT CO.
Home of the German-American Co., 3152 Gratiot, Detroit, established by a heel-clicking Prussian, one Thaddeus Marian Adalbert Donaj (Ted Donay), in 1935. The business name was changed when World War II was declared. A couple of truck loads of records were hauled from here after Donay's arrest by the FBI. He was a cohort of Max Stephans. FBI photo.

1942 he was 42 years old, divorced, and living in Centerline, Michigan, next to Detroit. He had a young son. His marriage had broken up because of his authoritarian attitude. His wife had confided to friends that she could not tolerate his strict rules and his overbearing conduct.

Donay must have visualized himself as a Prussian nobleman. He stood ramrod straight and acted the part of the leader who expected to have his orders followed to the letter. It was as though he was trying to overcompensate for the Polish side of his background by out "Nazi-ing" the best of the Nazis. With his posturing and his impeccable European social graces, which seemed to be from another era, he could have been a comic figure. He was not comic. There was an ominous side to him.

He was a rabid anti-Semite. He followed Nazi party doctrine to the letter. President Roosevelt was referred to as "Rosenvelt" and was said to be Jewish and a part of the international Jewish plot to control the world's finances.

When the U.S. went to war against Germany, both Stephan and Donay purged the word "German" from their business names. Donay thought up a new name, the Europe Importing Company. Stephan, showing less imagination, simply and quickly covered up the word "German" with a crude splotch of paint, making the name of his establishment, henceforth, "Restaurant."

The funds of Donay's business were frozen but the place was still a focal point for people sending food and money orders to Germany. It was generally felt, though not directly proved, that even during the war Donay had ways of making contacts in Germany. When he was arrested the FBI would fill a two ton panel truck, twice, with documents and articles from his business. A sampling of those artifacts gives some insight into his character and allegiance. For example, there was a phonograph record of a popular German hit of the day, "*Wir Fahren Gegen England*" (We are Going Against England). There was also a deck of anti-Semetic playing cards and a copy of an anti-Semetic Christmas poem which went as follows;

"Out of the west came three wise men,
Levy, Goldberg, and Uncle Ben,
Chanting 'Hark the Herald Angels Sing
See Cohen and Ginsberg for a diamond ring.'
For the Christians were born for Christmas day,
But Goldberg will give you 6 months to pay (plus 10%).
Oh Little Star of Bethlehem,
For Christmas gifts see Abraham.
And when the Herald Angels loom
Order your turkey from Rosenbloom.
Get your Christmas tree of pine
But buy your bells from Silverstein.
Down the chimney Santa comes,

With a load of toys from Isaac Blum's.
Ring out the old, ring in the new
But your money goes to some foxy Jew.
After peace on earth and good will to many
You can hock your watch with Uncle Benny.
Silent Night, Holy Night,
Darned if I don't think Hitler was right."

The FBI's collection included 10,000 small cards with that poem printed on them. Donay distributed them at every opportunity.

In addition, there was a letter to Donay from one of his sisters in Germany. There was indication that she was employed as a clerk somewhere in the office of the *Reichsmarschall* himself, Hermann Goering. Donay had another sister who was married to the Polish ambassador to Estonia. His brother, Felix, had been a partner with him in the business but had quit due to bad health.

The business netted Donay about $3,000 per year in income, $60 per week, or about half what Richard Bertelmann made as a supervisor in the war plant. It was interesting that Donay cared to work in his dark little store for that small wage. With his education and experience he could have easily earned twice as much, or more. We can only surmise that he preferred the freedom of movement that the store allowed. Also, he could pick his own social status rather than have it set for him by his position in a factory.

That Donay was influential in the community of Nazi sympathizers can be best shown by small incidents. For example, once, another German-American had just returned from Germany where he had gone to claim a modest inheritance. The Nazi government had levied a tax on it, which the man had, somehow, avoided when he brought the inheritance back to the U.S. He told this to Donay in a rather smug manner, adding that the Nazis would have a tough time ever getting their money. Donay was disturbed by the man's anti-Nazi attitude and convinced him that the Nazis had ways of reaching to any corner of the world to get what was owed to them. The man was so convinced that Donay was speaking the truth that he withdrew all the inheritance from the bank and put it in a postal money order.

Another time Donay conducted a sort of kangaroo court, although the accused was not in attendance. In May 1940, a certain Frederich Schreiner was in Donay's store in the presence of Donay's brother Felix and Dietrich Rintelin, the store clerk. Schreiner said that he heard a mutual acquaintance by the name of Emil Leidich say, "I hope they kill Hitler, that son of a bitch." The group in the store was shocked by the remark. Donay wrote a memo attesting to the statement and even asked his clerk to sign it. The clerk refused. It was believed that Donay's intent was to send the memo to Germany and, in fact, he may have.

Donay did permit one American custom to intrude on his Prussian lifestyle. His close friends, including Max Stephan, called him by the American nickname for Theodore. To them, he was "Ted."

The other half of the Stephan family was Agnes, who was nine years younger than Max. She had been 13 when the First World War started and remembered the bombing of her native Cologne. She had seven sisters and four brothers back in Germany, with whom she had lost contact in 1942. Before her marriage she had worked as a clerk in a grocery store and had earned money as a seamstress. Her philosophies, if they could be called that, closely paralleled those of Max and Donay. A story was told about her that illustrated, in part, her beliefs. She was once purchasing a trivial personal item, it may have been a pair of gloves, and she detected that the store clerk was Jewish. She berated the clerk and demanded to be waited on by a non-Jewish employee.

While that story reflects her anti-Semitism, it should be noted that anti-Semetism was not uniquely German. Anti-Semitism was commonly practiced in America by non-Germans, and was an institutionalized part of life at that time. I must frankly admit to my own prejudices and those of my family, then. I know that an aunt of mine in New York made remarks to Jews that were as insulting as those of Agnes Stephan. Likewise, all Germans need not be painted with the brush of anti-Semitism. During the hijacking of an airliner by Arab terrorists in 1985, a German flight attendant hid the passports of passengers with Jewish sounding names.

As for Agnes, she tended to be bossy and, more and more, was directing the business affairs of the restaurant. Sometime during 1941 Max finally insisted that she stay out of the running of the business. There were signs of trouble in the marriage.

Before the U.S. entered the war, Max and his circle of friends were outspoken in their pro-German sentiments. They believed and hoped that Germany would overrun Russia and that Japan would overrun India. England would then be forced to quit. Those were hopes that were close to realities at the time.

In any event, on December 7, 1941 the Japanese, who apparently had not consulted with Max and his friends, or even with Hitler, spoiled things by attacking Pearl Harbor and bringing the U.S. into the war. America's entry into the war cut the bottom out from under Max's dreams but the out of step life continued, more quietly. Packages were still sent to the prisoners in Canada and the German societies still met. In the latter part of December, 1941 Stephan did buy a $100 U.S. War Bond.

In April, 1942, the Stephans had operated the Detroit restaurant for nine years. Their home continued to be the living quarters upstairs. They had no children but they shared their home with Arnold, their pet chow.

Max could gloat some over his successful maneuvers to outwit the law. And those minor liquor violations in Windsor, well, they were nothing. It may have been that a feeling of overconfidence was developing. He was aware that the FBI and the immigration authorities were watching him. He had been warned by a two people, one of whom was a friend named Anders Hammelef.

Hammelef was the salesman for Lowenbrau beer and called on Stephan about twice a month from mid-1936 until November 1940. He became friends with the Stephans and in fact liked them, a fact that he actually admitted to the FBI. In early 1942 Max told Hammelef that the man who cleaned beer coils at the restaurant had been picked up by the FBI. Max went on to say that the beer coil cleaner (his name is not known) had been told by someone at the Immigration Department to warn Max that he would be the next one to be picked up. Hammelef said to Max, "For God's sake, what in the hell have you been doing?"

Max said to him, "Nothing that could be wrong." He told Hammelef that he had sent a number of packages to the prisoners in Canada but after Pearl Harbor he had gone to the FBI and asked them about it and they said that as long as the Post Office would accept the mail, then it was perfectly legal. He also claimed to have sent cigars and cigarettes to the boys in the hospital at Battle Creek, a large POW camp in Michigan. Hammelef claimed that Max said he would never do anything to harm the U.S.

In 1942, the FBI office in Detroit was having a busy year. In addition to arrests for espionage and failure to register as an enemy alien, 120 raids had been conducted on the homes of Germans and Italians. They had collected flags, guns, cameras, binoculars, and shortwave radios, all of which could not legally be kept by aliens.

One thing was certain, by then the FBI was watching Max Stephan and his friends very closely.

Chapter 5

Peter Krug's Journey

Peter Krug was born in Munich, Germany on April 18, 1920. It was a birth date that would place him at an ideal age to be a part of the plans of Adolph Hitler.

In 1924 the Krug family moved to Chemnitz, an industrial city near the Czechoslovakian boarder. It is 250 miles east of Cologne where, in 1924, Max Stephan left the German National Police and opened his *bierstube.*

At six, Peter Krug entered school and at 17, in 1937, he had completed the standard German education of the thirties. It was roughly equivalent to the completion of high school in the U.S. Following that, he attended military leader's school for six months. By then Hitler had long since risen to power as the head of the German Government and dreams of world conquest were starting to become reality.

In late 1938, after Hitler annexed Czechoslovakia's Sudetenland, Krug joined the *Luftwaffe.* Krug's training continued during the time when Czechoslovakia, and later Poland, fell.

In 1940, when France fell, Krug completed his *Luftwaffe* training and was promoted to the rank of *Leutnant*, equivalent to a U.S. Second Lieutenant. He was presented with his commission by Hermann Goering, the *Reichsmarschall* himself, who shook hands with Krug and the other graduates in the ceremony. Krug was assigned to KG 3 (*Kampfgeschwader* 3, literally Battle Group 3). His unit flew two-engine Dornier Do 17Z bombers. The British called those planes the "flying pencil" because of their thin fuselage, which also dictated a small bomb load of 2,200 pounds. The bomber was an old standby in the *Luftwaffe* and was a model that had been used in the Spanish Civil War. Its shape was such that it was sometimes confused with the British Hampden bomber, a fact that sometimes caused those British planes to be fired on by their own anti-aircraft guns. The Dornier's vulnerability was well known to the RAF. It was weak in defensive fire, particularly below and from the rear.

With the fall of France, Hitler assembled his invasion fleet for the assault on England. This was the Battle of Britain, starting in August of 1940. By the end of August both sides were suffering heavy losses.

On August 28 Peter Krug was part of a major *Luftwaffe* assault on two airfields. At about 8 A.M. they left their French airfields. Krug's unit in their Do 17Z's headed for Rochford and another unit flying Heinkels, headed for Eastchurch. They were protected by 120 fighters.

Krug's crew consisted of the Observer, *Gefreiter* Arthur Burghardt, *Gefreiter* Willi Gailer whose job is unclear now, and *Flieger* Anton Bruckmann who was Gunner. Both *Gefreiters* had a machine gun to operate, in addition to any other duties. Incidently, the rank of *Flieger* is the lowest rank, like private or airman in the U.S. service. The *Gefreiters* were the next rank higher and were equivalent to Privates First Class in the U.S. service or Lance Corporals in the British Army. Incidently, Hitler is sometimes called an ex-Corporal, when referring to his World War I rank. Actually, he was a *Gefrieter*, but since the British equivalent is a Lance Corporal, he has commonly been called an ex-Corporal.

On their way home from the mission, Krug and his crew were attacked by a Spitfire believed to be of Number 54 Squadron. All four were wounded and both of the thundering, 1,000 horsepower, Bramo 323 engines were hit. At 12:24 in the afternoon Krug made a forced landing just off the shore of England, near Foreness Point, Thanet, where the south shore of the Thames estuary meets the Strait of Dover. An unconfirmed story was told that his crew shot down their attacker and that he was picked up by the Germans.

In any event, Peter Krug became one of the many prisoners

of war that England was acquiring. He was wounded in the right hand and right eye and was sent to Woolwich Hospital where he underwent an eye operation. By September 7 he was sufficiently recovered to be released from the hospital and was sent to one of the POW camps in England.

Four months later, on January 6, 1941, he was transferred to Canada in a boatload of "Battle of Britain" prisoners. At Halifax he and the others met their hosts, the Veterans' Guard and the long train ride began. The Guards were not supposed to have any casual conversation with the prisoners, but the prisoners were able to glean scraps of information. They began to learn that their destination was somewhere north of Lake Superior, actually Camp W, but they did not yet know the name.[1]

Then about midway through the journey Krug's companion, von Werra, made his successful dive through the train window. Krug wanted to follow him but there was no time and he went on with the rest to Camp W. They arrived in the dead of winter and it was the most desolate, cold, and snow covered place they had ever seen. The buildings were old army barracks that had somehow lost their doors. Worse yet were the guards. They were not the regular Veterans' Guard but instead were Canadian Indians, specially hired for the job. It just didn't seem like the Canadians were playing fair. The prisoners learned very quickly that the Indians were quick on the trigger, ill tempered, and seldom gave quarter in the sporting manner of the English. At least that was how they documented it themselves.[10]

The senior prisoner was Lt. Col. Hasso von Wedel whose story, by itself, was intriguing. In the first World War he had flown in Baron von Richthofen's, The Red Baron's, squadron. When von Richthofen was killed, the squadron command was given to Hermann Goering. Young von Wedel was given the job of introducing Goering to each of the squadron pilots when Goering arrived at their airfield to take command. Between the wars von Wedel was a history professor and was actually too old for active service in World War II. However, due to his experience he received an appointment as *Luftwaffe* historian during the Battle of Britain. In his assignment he was not supposed to fly, but this ran counter to his Prussian military instincts. Somehow, he convinced his nephew, Squadron Commander Lützow, to at least let him fly a plane. He was shot down over England, and crash-landed, killing a farm boy in the process. The boy's mother gave von Wedel a cup of tea in her kitchen while the troops were coming for him. The experience affected him deeply and created in him a very great appreciation for the English. As a prisoner in Canada he later became seriously ill and was eventually exchanged. It is not certain but he may have been killed in the last days of the war, in the fighting in Berlin.[10]

Von Wedel led the prisoners in a hunger strike and gained doors on the barracks and a few other concessions.

Discouraging news was received by the grapevine from a nearby enlisted men's camp. Twenty escapees from that camp had been trapped in an abandoned logging camp and it was said that four were shot down in cold blood.

Bad news of another kind reached the camp in June of 1941 when the prisoners learned that Hitler had invaded Russia. Their hopes for an early release were fading fast.

Then one of the Camp W prisoners developed an escape plan. He was *Oberleutnant* Müller and he decided to fake a stomach ulcer so that he could be sent to a nearby hospital. He escaped from there and for three days nothing was heard of him. On the evening of the third day the prisoners could hear shouts from the Indians. Someone said, "They have him, 28 days in the tank (the close-confinement, punishment cell), for sure," that being the normal punishment for escape. The next day Müller was carried in. He had been shot in the forehead and to the prisoners it looked like murder.

After that the prisoners felt they had a duty to carry a first hand account of Müller's and the four enlisted men's deaths, back to Germany. Then in October and November of 1941 the Bowmanville Boy's Reformatory near Toronto, was converted to a POW camp and the Camp W prisoners were moved there. November 22 was the actual date of transfer for Peter Krug.

Among the prisoners were "Americanologists" like Reinhart

Pfundtner, Walter Manhart and "Doc" Wagner. Pfundtner, the Berlin hockey star, had been an exchange student in Massachusetts. Doc had been a ski instructor at an American resort hotel. He had saved his money and used it to become a lawyer in Vienna. The Germans sometimes call a lawyer "Doktor". They could give valuable information to others. It was important, for example, to know the proper way to hitchhike in America, "Hold your thumb at eye level."[10]

The move from Camp W to Bowmanville was not without incident. Three prisoners, Manhart, Waller, and Malischewski had escaped from the train. They had been recaptured by the Mounted Police and were delivered to Bowmanville in handcuffs. At the end of November, 1941, they were in the Bowmanville tank. That was about the time that the prisoners received the news of von Werra's death. On the same day, November 23, Ulrich Steinhilper was ready to escape. He was the one who had made sticks to hold up the wire. When no one was looking he slipped under the fence. Although he was spotted almost immediately, he was out of sight before he could be stopped. He ran, walked, and hopped trains to the U.S. border at Niagara Falls. He had memorized the names of some people in Buffalo that he would try to contact. This was still before the U.S. was in the war, so the border represented comparative freedom. On the final leg of his trip he hid on a locomotive. The train crossed the Niagara gorge to the American side, but before he could jump off without being seen, it backed up and returned to Canada. He was caught back on the Canadian side and sent, frozen stiff, to a jail for temporary safekeeping. Reporters interviewed him and wrote accounts of a cowering, stammering Nazi. He was infuriated when he later read the accounts back in Bowmanville. He was in such bad shape that he was not given the usual 28 days of detention in the "tank."[10]

Two weeks later the U.S. and Germany were at war. For the prisoners, that created a great deal of uncertainty. No one really knew what the reception might be from people who were sympathetic enough to send packages but might not want to become involved in what would now be a serious crime.

In spite of the uncertainty and the adverse weather, plans

proceeded. Manhart was released from the tank, from his earlier escape and Steinhilper asked to borrow his prize possession, a pair of wire cutters. Using them in December, 1941, he escaped again. Manhart had insisted that the wire cutters be tossed back after cutting through the wire. The toss was short and the cutters hit the warning wire and bounced back into the forbidden zone. Generally there was a main fence and an inner fence about 15 feet inside. The space between the fences was the "dead man's" zone—the area which kept the prisoners away from the main fence. Manhart reached into the dead man's zone and retrieved the cutters but was caught by the Canadians in what appeared to be his own escape attempt. He went back to the tank only three days after having left it. He had saved the wire cutters, however, by passing them to another prisoner.[10]

In eight days Steinhilper was back again. He had been recaptured in Montreal and he and Manhart were then in adjoining detention cells. Steinhilper had learned a lesson the hard way, on that escape. He had written down the names of people who had sent packages, and carried the list with him. The list was found by the Mounted Police when he was captured. He realized, then, that he had implicated people who possibly would not even have helped him. He went to great lengths to give his word on that point to the Mounted Police, but of course, he had no way of knowing if anything was ever done to them. In all future escapes, he memorized the names that he had, and it appears that he influenced the others to do the same.

Actually the detention cells, where Manhart and Steinhilper were held, were outside the camp proper. The German mess sergeant smuggled some items to Manhart, including a saw made from a knife. Using it, Manhart cut away the floorboards to escape again. That time he got to the U.S. and spent New Year's Day with a Quaker family who helped him, thinking only that he was a stranger in need of help. He was recaptured soon after.[10]

Those brief experiences led prisoners to develop a complex plan that Peter Krug would use. They saw clearly that the swift detection of their escape and absence was a major factor in their early recapture. What was needed was a more elaborate plan that would give the escapees time to get far from the camp before their absence was noticed. That required two things; escape must be accomplished without leaving visible signs of exit and their absence must be covered up in the roll call.

A prisoner named Waller probably deserved the credit for one of the important parts of the next plan. At his suggestion, two dummies would be made using uniforms stuffed with straw. The heads would be made from flour and water with detailed facial features painted on. Since the prisoners were only counted in groups, the dummies, which could actually stand on their own, would each be positioned between two prisoners and would make the count come out correctly.

Steinhilper and Waller were to benefit from the dummies first. They noted that Canadian workmen frequently climbed over the fences on ladders while making repairs. They decided to pose as workmen in coveralls while Pfundtner posed as a Veterans' Guard sergeant in a fake uniform that could not possibly stand close inspection. On February 27, 1942 they went through their act. Wearing workmen's coveralls and carrying paint and homemade ladders they were escorted past the warning wire by Pfundtner. Under his direction they proceeded to paint yellow rings around the fence posts. They gradually worked over an area and maneuvered themselves outside the camp. Once there, they actually sat down on the grass and smoked a cigarette amidst their paint cans, brushes, and ladders.[10]

As planned, after they were gone for three days the prisoners hid the dummies and let the count come up short. The escapees should have had enough distance by then and the dummies could and would be used again.

Leaving the camp, Steinhilper and Waller had made their way to Watertown, N.Y. where they were recaptured on March 6. That was the case in which one of them had aroused the suspicion of a policeman when he mispronounced "Carthage", N.Y., their next destination.[10]

Peter Krug and a prisoner named Erich Boehle prepared to be the next to use the dummies. Since the "workmen" trick had not been discovered, it too, would be repeated. Their plans had begun much earlier. Peter Krug had started his preparations when he arrived at Bowmanville. Each prisoner had been photographed for his official camp identification record. There were older photos of the prisoners, the ones taken shortly after capture. However, the prisoners were usually in a state of near shock then, and better resemblances were needed. To prepare for his new picture Krug first had his hair trimmed close to the sides of his head so that the skin showed well above the ears. Though he did not wear glasses, he borrowed a pair to wear for the photo. He was quite pleased with the result and felt that he looked like a recruit. In early 1942, with his hair long, and without the glasses, there was little resemblance between him and his official photo.[10]

The preparation of a more specific escape plan and cover identity had also been started earlier. In February of 1942 the French liner, Normandie had been taken over by the U.S. Maritime Commission for refitting in New York Harbor. It was to be converted into a troop ship. In the process, a worker with a cutting torch was removing an ornamental fixture from a salon wall. Sparks from the torch fell into a pile of life preservers, starting the catastrophic fire that gutted the ship. When the fire was finally out the Normandie was on its side in the water and was nothing more than a derelict.

The newspapers, including those allowed inside Bowmanville, were very specific in their details of the catastrophe. There were cutaway drawings, plans, photos, and the names of many of the ship's officers.

The document makers at Bowmanville, probably two prisoners named Kauter and Strehl, went to work. They had developed considerable skill at forgery. With crude tools they could copy company letterheads from newspaper ads, they could duplicate a rubber stamp by using a hard boiled egg, and they were quite proud of their U.S. Selective Service cards. Peter Krug was to become Jean Etté a carpenter or joiner from the Normandie.[10] He would carry with him a firm job offer from the F.R. Larkin Company in Windsor, Ontario. Also, two other letters were prepared, the first of which, in French, read as follows;

> Jean Etté
> Date of Birth: Jan. 17, 1917
> Place of Birth: Strasbourg, France
> Profession: Joiner
>
> This is to certify that Mr. Jean Etté was on board the S.S. Normandie until Dec. 12, 1941. Upon the turning over of the S.S. Normandie to the American Maritime Commission Mr. Jean Etté has been dismissed. His sailing papers are deposited with the Consul General of France in New York City.
>
> signed/ P.F. Pennault
> 1st Officer S.S. Normandie

The second letter was supposedly from the Postmaster of New York City. It read;

> Postmaster General
> New York City
>
> It is stated herewith that Mr. Jean Etté, a French subject, has applied in time for his alien registration card. It will be issued to him in due course. Mr. Jean Etté is entitled to stay in the U.S. for the duration of the war. Then he has to apply for American citizenship or leave the country. His sailing papers are deposited with the Consulate General of France in New York City.

The papers were good, but an experienced customs agent would probably have recognized them as forgeries.

In any event, Peter Krug, who actually had a very limited knowledge of French, was to be the Frenchman, Jean Etté. His English was good, however, and that was what was important. He memorized all the facts of the Normandie disaster from the papers; the names, the floorplans, all that was available. Erich Boehle, 28 years old, would be the other "workman" and would escape with him. Boehle was to pose as a free

Norwegian flyer. That solved a lot of problems in respect to his accent, even though a knowledgeable person could certainly detect the difference between English spoken with a German accent compared to a Norwegian accent.

In spite of the elaborate preparations, they still had little money and would have to get by on their wits until they could find someone who would help them. For escape clothes they would simply continue to wear their coveralls, stolen from camp workmen.

In early afternoon on Wednesday, April 15, 1942, a soccer game was purposely scheduled as a distraction for the guards. The referee called both teams together and explained that an escape was planned. The players were asked to stage a game that would draw the guards' attention. When the referee blew three short blasts on his whistle, whoever had the ball was supposed to kick it over the fence.[10]

Play began and Krug and Boehle, their hair colored gray, came out, carrying a ladder, from behind some buildings. They put it in place and climbed over into the path between the two rows of fences. They pretended to make repairs and soon, two guards making their rounds headed their way. The signal was given and the ball went over the fence. The prisoners shouted for the guards to return it. One of the guards kicked it a few times and threw it back. The prisoners cheered in appreciation and continued their game. The guards continued on their way, past Krug and Boehle.

At half time the players could see Krug and Boehle disappear over some distant hills. The two walked to a nearby railway and waited for the first freight train bound toward Toronto. They hopped on and rode on the outside of a car. They arrived in a Toronto freight yard at dark. There, Boehle thought he had a better idea and jumped into an open box car. Just as Krug was about to follow him, two men came along the track. Krug hid behind some bushes and saw the two men close the door, throw the latch, and walk on. Almost immediately, the train started and Krug, when it was safe, ran alongside, trying to keep up with Boehle. Finally, he jumped on a car with a load of logs. When it stopped, he got off and ran among the cars calling out for Boehle. Eventually, he had to give up. It was late at night, and in the confusion of switching, it was a hopeless job. Unquestionably he had made a valiant effort to locate his comrade who, he thought, was locked inside the box car.[10]

Krug found the passenger depot, went inside and fell asleep. He was in Toronto's main railway station, a busy place during the war.[7] It was the next day, the 16th, when he was awakened by a railway employe, a gate man, named George Billings. He quickly tried to apologize and act like it was a mistake, which in a way it was. Billings did not seem to be suspicious. There had been no calls from Bowmanville, or anywhere else. Eventually Krug explained that he was going to Windsor. Billings explained that it was unfortunate because the Windsor train did not leave until 11 P.M. that night. He suggested that a bus might be better.

Krug could see that the conversation, innocent though it appeared, was probing more deeply into his identity. Finally, Billings asked Krug if he was a stranger and he knew he must recite his Normandie cover story. When he was part way through the story, Billings called Corporal Albert Pearce of the Military Police, to hear the rest of it.

After hearing part of the story, Corporal Pearce asked Krug to accompany him to his office where he examined the papers. Since Pearce did not read French, Krug translated the one letter for him from memory, not really understanding French either. For Krug it was the luck of the draw. Had Pearce spoken French, he undoubtedly would have used it and Krug would have been exposed. He would have been back in Bowmanville for supper that evening.

Pearce looked through a card file and finally turned to Krug with a smile. He had satisfied himself, and said, "So you want to go to Windsor? Well, I can't give you any money but I know someone who will help you." He told Krug of a priest at the Catholic Adjustment Bureau and asked if Krug was a Catholic. This was something that Krug had not anticipated, but he knew in an instant that as a phoney Frenchman he must also be a phoney Catholic.[10]

The Corporal made an introductory call to the priest and then gave Krug his address. Krug left the station and debated with himself about the appointment he had. Should he go to the priest or not? The priest's name was McGrath, but he might well be bilingual. If it came down to using French it would be the end for Krug.[10]

He recalled an uncle of his who had spent 15 years in New Zealand. When he returned to Germany for a visit he had almost forgotten his German. Unless the priest used French regularly, he probably would not be conversant in it. It looked like he should take a chance, he really had nothing else.

As it turned out it was no problem. Krug met the priest, Father M.J. McGrath, who suggested that if it was alright with Krug they would converse in English, "So that my secretary can understand."

Once again Krug told the Normandie story and even felt some minor guilt pangs, deceiving the kindly priest. By then it was dinner time on the 16th and Krug was invited to join the priest and his secretary for the meal. Afterwards, the secretary drove Krug to the bus station, bought his ticket to Windsor, and gave him $1.25.[10]

Krug had one minor scare during the bus ride. The driver apparently mistakenly thought that Krug's ticket was for some intermediate point on the way to Windsor. When Krug stayed on past that point, the driver came back and double-checked his ticket. Everything was in order, of course, but for Krug it was a heart stopper, just for a few minutes.[7]

Krug arrived in Windsor while it was still dark, early in the morning of Friday, the 17th, and began to plan his crossing of the Detroit River. Wandering along the shore that morning he saw an old rowboat. He went to a nearby store and bought some fruit, cigarettes, and a paper. Then he found a hiding place in some bushes along the river. He shaved in a puddle and sat down to eat the fruit and read the paper. In it he read of Boehle's capture the previous day, and also saw his own picture, the one with the glasses and the white sidewall haircut.[10]

Boehle had not fared too badly. When his box car stopped

moving he simply threw the lever, opened the door, and jumped out. He was unable to find Krug and simply jumped back into another car. He rode the train all the way to Niagara Falls, New York, having crossed the border apparently on the outside of a train. He was recaptured at about 10:15 A.M. and after about 3 hours of grilling, admitted who he was. The police had permitted him to bathe and clean the soot off himself before questioning. There was little doubt about how he had crossed to the U.S. American authorities noted that he was carrying forged papers that identified him as a Royal Norwegian Air Force officer.[7] Newspaper articles said that he and Krug had cut through the wire to escape.

Actually, things had unravelled a bit back at Bowmanville. The dummy trick had been discovered the previous day, about 2 hours before Boehle was caught. At that time, Captain Richmond Henry Atkey, the Camp Dental Officer who incidentally had worked on Krug's teeth not long before, had administered the count of prisoners. The actual count was accomplished by Staff Sergeant Cecil J. Rule, the senior noncom in the enclosure. As he walked past the ranks of prisoners he noticed the two dummies. They were good, but not that good. The faces simply had too much red paint on them. He made believe he miscounted and went back to start over. That time when he was abreast of one dummy, he grabbed it. The prisoners destroyed the other one. All that was known then was that two prisoners were missing. Captain Greenwood, the Adjutant, sent for the civilian interpreter and preparations were made for an identification parade. That was the lengthy process in which the prisoners were supposed to line up in alphabetical order to be compared with their official identification photo. It was an arduous task because the prisoners customarily did everything possible to impede its progress.

About the time that was happening, Boehle was caught. Eventually it was established that prisoner number 52021, Peter Krug, was missing.

The alarm went out to police in both Canada and the U.S. and border surveillance was increased. The FBI prepared a wanted poster, the first of its kind during the war.

On Friday, April 17th, Krug continued to sit out the day in his hiding place. In the afternoon he made himself a paddle. Then, all he could do was look across the river at Detroit and wonder about what kind of reception he would receive now that the U.S. was at war. He had memorized 15 addresses in the U.S. Four were in Detroit and the others were in Chicago and New York.

About 11 P.M. that night he launched "his" rowboat and started across the Detroit River, paddling from the bow. About half way across, the paddle broke and, using a few choice words from his vocabulary, threw it away. He could see border patrol boats with their searchlights shining on the shoreline. Once, he crouched down in his boat until a patrol boat turned and went by. He used the light on the top of the Penobscot Building as a beacon and eventually landed on the U.S. side of the river.

He did not know it at first but he had landed in the U.S. on Belle Isle, an island park, connected to Detroit by a single bridge. It was after midnight when he landed and it was his 22nd birthday, April 18, 1942.

As Krug began to move about and explore the vicinity of his U.S. landfall he realized that he was on an island. Finally, he found the bridge and walked its half mile length to the mainland. Coincidentally, Stephan's restaurant was near the end of that bridge, but he would not meet the man until later in the day.

For the rest of the night Krug slept in the doorway, from which he was chased early in the morning. As he had done in Windsor, he bought a paper and found his picture and story on the third page. He next killed some time so that he would not call on anyone too early.

It was a matter of sheer luck that the area along East Jefferson, where he had landed, was also the location of the people whose names he had memorized. He cautiously asked passersby for directions. At the first address no one was home. At the second, the people had moved. At the third, a small girl answered an looked at him suspiciously, he thought, and he left.

DETROIT, MICHIGAN
Detroit skyline at night as seen from Windsor, Canada. Note the light atop the Penobscot Building which served as a guide for Krug as he paddled across the Detroit River from E. Windsor to Belle Isle.

Then, close to 9:00 A.M. he made the contact with Mrs. Bertelmann on Philip Street. Mrs. Bertelmann was still in her robe, getting ready to get dressed for a trip downtown. Her husband and daughter were at work.

Upstairs in Mrs. Bertelmann's kitchen he identified himself by pulling an officer's epaulet out from the inside of his coveralls and saying in German, "I come from Canada, I am Peter Krug." Mrs. Bertelmann had read of him in the papers and was terrified. She felt chilled, her legs gave way, and she held on to the wall for support. Krug had already decided that he would give her 10 seconds and if she did not say anything he would leave. He could see the same paper on the table, that he had read that morning. Before the 10 seconds were up she regained

BELLE ISLE BRIDGE
Bridge where Krug walked across from Belle Isle to E. Jefferson Ave., Detroit, after he landed on Belle Isle about 1:00 A.M. on April 18, 1942. FBI photo.

her composure and put her hand on his arm in what he felt was a motherly gesture. She asked why he had come to her and how he had been able to do what he did. Then she noticed how young he was and asked him his age. He said he was 22 on that very day. She was surprised and said, "Twenty two and your birthday and you did all those things as the paper reported."[10]

As he explained his need for help, she began to realize her predicament. "Naturally I will help," she said, adding that she should call the police. Then she realized that her guest might be hungry and seated him at the kitchen table while she started a pot of coffee.

While it was heating she called Clifford 1258, the number of Max Stephan, the only person she could think of who could

BERTELMANN HOME

Mrs. Bertelmann's home (upstairs) at 259 Philip St., Detroit. This is where the escaped German bomber pilot made his first contact in Detroit. FBI photo.

possibly help. The phone in the restaurant was downstairs. At that time of day, the only person downstairs was an employee named "Joe" who Stephan referred to as a "flunky," who was cleaning up at the time, in preparation for the day's business. Joe answered the phone and said that Max Stephan had not come down yet. Mrs. Bertelmann left urgent word for him to call. Krug asked, "Who is Stephan?"

While the coffee was still heating she served Krug some cheese, sardines, bread, and crackers. He ate some, but his stomach became upset and he had to stop. In half an hour Stephan called back. Mrs. Bertelmann said, "Come over quick, something terrible has happened." He replied, "Don't you know I'm busy." In desperation she blurted out the reason and quickly hung up.

In what seemed like just a few minutes, Max was there. The front door was still open and he came bounding up, along with Arnold, the chow. He entered the kitchen where Krug was seated and said, "That must be Lieutenant Krug," and at the same time held out his hand, adding, "My name is Stephan." He made one comment about the impossibility of what Krug was attempting to do, suggesting that maybe Krug should give himself up. Krug said, "I have to try it."

Mrs. Bertelmann was still in her robe and went into the bedroom to get dressed, but listened to the conversation through the door. The menfolk went into the living room to talk. Stephan sat in a chair with his hands on the upper parts of his thighs and smiled as he listened and talked, occasionally slapping his thighs with glee. After all, he had pulled off a few himself. It did not take Krug long to develop a distrust of Stephan. Krug could not really understand what made the man tick. He seemed to be an American, a German-American, but in the mixing of the two nationalities he had somehow retained the worst of both, Krug felt. In later years Krug said that the man seemed to have the simplemindedness of a small town German with the brashness of an American businessman all rolled into one. He was not happy with this new friend and under different circumstances he would have dropped him. They were certainly not social equals.

Stephan soon learned of the birthday and told Krug that he was to come with him and that a birthday party was in order.

"How long since you have been in a bar?"

"How long since you have seen a pretty girl?"

Krug could only answer, "Oh God . . . "

"We will catch up on everything, my boy, everything," Stephan said, laughing.[10]

Politely, Krug declined, pointing out the danger to everyone. "I would rather not, Mr. Stephan," he said.

Stephan replied, "What? Afraid of pretty girls? A daring flier like you?" Then Stephan made a suggestion that really made Krug doubt the man's sanity. He said, "You stay with me until the day after tomorrow (Monday, April 20). Tomorrow evening we have our club meeting, all Germans. You will give a fine lecture about Germany, your experiences, your escape, and so forth."[10]

It was insane of course and Krug must have thought that he had fallen in with an idiot. The thought of attending such a meeting in the heart of Detroit, in wartime, was outrageous.

Krug still knew that he had nothing else going for him. He politely declined the meeting, hoping to get some help and move on as quickly as possible. His decision to miss the club meeting turned out to be a good one.

Stephan was disappointed and Krug apologized. But Stephan put the matter behind him quickly and suggested a new idea. He would at least show the flier a good time for the day and Krug agreed with the new plan. Before leaving Mrs. Bertelmann's the subject of Krug's clothing came up. She was preparing a package for Canada and happened to have some things handy. They went through the pile of castoffs and selected some underwear, socks and shoes. Krug would continue to wear the coveralls. Lastly, Stephan used a bit of connivance to get some money from Mrs. Bertelmann, and thereby get her more deeply involved. He explained that he had come away without any money, which wasn't really a problem, since he was going right back to the restaurant, and suggested that she contribute something to help Krug in his travels. She produced a $20 bill, later explaining that she put it on the table and did not see who took it. Krug was to give a more forthright version.

Before noon Krug was seated in Stephan's Chevrolet and the two were headed for the restaurant. Meanwhile, Mrs. Bertelmann was busy in her basement, burning Krug's old shoes in the furnace.

Chapter 6

"One of Meier's Boys"

We can probably assume that Saturday, April 18, 1942, was about like any other day at Stephan's Restaurant on Jefferson Avenue. When Max came down the stairs and received the urgent message to call Mrs. Bertelmann, well, it could have been something about the sausage for Schwaben Society meeting. He called back immediately and at first balked at going over until she blurted out the reason.

After meeting Krug, Stephan was vastly impressed and must have been able to see all sorts of possibilities for him to enhance his standing in his circle of friends. After all, there were those who looked down on him, failed to take him seriously, and regarded him as a dumbhead and even a buffoon. For the day he would introduce Krug to his acquaintances, visit bars, and maybe become good friends. He could be like a father to the boy.

As they drove back along Jefferson to the restaurant, Stephan's mind was already plotting. Upon reaching the restaurant he drove around the back, telling Krug to get out and walk around the front. Stephan then let himself in through the back door and went to the front door to unlock it and greet his first customer of the day as if he had never seen him before. Inside the restaurant the two chatted some more. Krug told more of his plans and his desire to reach South America. He said he had the address of a woman in Chicago who he thought would help him. Stephan promised to work on transportation to Chicago, but first, he said, he had some business of his own to attend to.

So that Krug would not become too bored while he, Stephan, was working, he suggested that Krug go for a little walk downtown and entertain himself for a while—just the kind of suggestion that must have appealed to a hunted fugitive who had barely slept in the past three days. Nevertheless, Krug listened to Stephan's instructions on how to find downtown Detroit and his suggestions on what to do when he got there. He left the restaurant and was on his own for a while. Outside the restaurant, he noticed the U.S. Rubber Company plant nearby. He walked downtown, bought some apples, and stared at the buildings like any tourist might do. When he was ready to return, instead of walking, he took a trolley and told the conductor to let him off at the Rubber Company.

Krug arrived back in the restaurant shortly after noon and found Stephan to be himself again. His previous commitments had been dispensed with and he said, "Now I have nothing to do and it is your birthday, we should celebrate." With that, Stephan reached into his pocket and brought out a gift, a wallet with some change in it, and a necktie. By then Stephan was becoming even more captivated by Krug and his exploits. Under questioning, Krug began to tell his host bits and pieces of his wartime experiences, both in Europe and Canada, and Stephan was entranced by it all. The next few hours became the highlight of the episode and Stephan, even if rating a failing grade in citizenship, certainly deserved an "A" for his entertainment efforts.

A busy afternoon began with the pair leaving the restaurant together and riding off in Stephan's car. The first stop was part business for Stephan. He stopped at the store of William C. Lenz who rented dishes, glassware, and crockery. Stephan needed those items the next day at the restaurant for the meeting of the Schwaben Society, the club meeting he had referred to earlier. Krug waited in the car. Stephan asked Lenz if he would call the railway station and inquire about trains to Chicago. Lenz, with no knowledge of Krug, called the station and got the information, relaying it to Stephan. "Trains," he said, "will leave for Chicago at 4 P.M. and 11 P.M. today." Carrying a box of dishes in his arms and an abbreviated train schedule in

A. W. LENZ CO.

On April 18, 1942, Stephan stopped at A. W. Lenz Co. to rent some dishes. Krug remained in Stephan's car parked at the curb. While at this store, Stephan made inquiry concerning train schedules to Chicago for Krug. FBI photo.

his head, Stephan returned to the car where Krug was waiting.

Next, the pair made a brief stop at a "Jew" store where Stephan bought a light traveling bag for Krug. It was tentatively planned that Krug would take the 4 P.M. train to Chicago, that afternoon. That still left time for some recreation.

Stephan next drove to Haller's Cafe at 1407 Randolph Street. August Haller, the proprietor, was a friend of Stephan's of some ten years. The bar was a flatiron-shaped place and at the time there were about 30 customers partaking of Haller's various libations. Stephan and Krug found a place at the bar and were waited on by Haller himself. He asked if Krug was

HALLER'S CAFE
Haller's where Krug was introduced as "one of Meier's boys." FBI photo.

21, the legal drinking age, and Stephan said, "Of course, or I wouldn't have brought him here, he's one of Meier's boys." (Meier may have been a mutual friend; nothing is known about him.) Haller served up Stephan's "usual"—boiler makers; whisky with a beer chaser. After a second round they left. Krug had begun, very quickly, to feel the drinks, and forgot his newly acquired bag, which he had carried into the bar with him. Haller had put it behind the bar, probably along with many other forgotten items. Krug remembered it as he was getting into the car and ran back in for it.

Next, they went to the Progressive Club, actually the Fortschrittbund Hall, at 3003 Elmwood. There were only about two patrons in the place, one of whom was a John McGuire, who could not have possibly had any Bund connections, except as a beer drinker. Stephan introduced Krug as "a

FORTSCHRITTSBUND HALL
Fortschrittsbund Hall, Detroit, where Stephan and Krug stopped for a few drinks on April 18, 1942. FBI photo.

flier friend from Milwaukee." The drinks had caused Krug to lapse into German and Stephan warned him to use only English. They had coffee and cake and washed it down with a schnapps before leaving. After they left, Emil the bartender said to McGuire, "Well that's the first time Max Stephan ever came in here without buying the house a drink." McGuire would later testify at Stephan's trial.

If Krug had doubts about Stephan at first, events were not doing much to improve things. "What was he?" Krug wondered. He seemed to alternate in his talk. He would brag about the freedom in America and then would switch over and drink a toast to a German military victory. Krug had simply never met anyone like Stephan in his life. It was now obvious that the man was unstable and the next stop was even more unsettling for Krug.[10]

From the Progressive Club they drove to the Europe Importing Company to see Theodore Donay. Stephan knew that Donay held him, Stephan, in rather low esteem while considering himself to be something of an aristocrat. It was most definitely a prestige enhancing visit. As they entered the store they were met by Dietrich Rintelin, Donay's clerk. Stephan brushed him aside saying, "This is nothing for you, today I want to see the boss." Donay came over and Rintelin went back to work, straightening and dusting merchandise. Stephan introduced Krug to Donay, telling him precisely who he was. Donay noted that his visitors were a little drunk and it irritated him somewhat, teetotaller that he was. Krug, particularly, had not held his liquor well and later admitted to being a little drunk. Under the circumstances, he was hardly qualified to match Stephan drink for drink.

Meanwhile, Rintelin was straining to hear the introduction. Krug's coveralls made him suspicious, they were simply not conventional street dress at the time. He could see the look on Donay's face which he later used four adjectives to describe; "startled, stunned, admiring, and smiling, as if he had just heard some interesting news." He heard the word "*lager*", the German word for camp, and then he heard someone in the trio say "$50,000", a number that was well known to Donay's circle of friends. It was, of course, the amount of bail that had been paid and forfeited by the German Consulate for von Werra.

As the redheaded Rintelin listened and tried his best to overhear, he gradually began to realize who the stranger was. His eavesdropping was even obvious to Krug who was becoming increasingly more nervous.

Donay asked Krug about conditions in Canada and Krug related the ordeals of Camp W and the shooting of Müller. Krug told Donay that one of his reasons for the escape was to get word of that back to Germany. There were implications at the time that in this contact, Krug had succeeded in accomplishing that objective. Donay contributed $20 toward fattening Krug's new wallet but as with many events of the day, a loss of memory accompanied the actual transfer of cash. It was even said that Krug, quite properly, tried to refuse the money, but Donay generously waved away Krug's polite refusal.

Shortly before they left, Stephan bought some German candy for Krug, out of Donay's stock. Donay later denied any knowledge of Krug's true identity. He did claim, however, that he was a student of accents and had noted that Krug, or whoever he was, spoke with a Saxon dialect.

Later Donay talked to Rintelin about the visit. If only, he remarked, Krug had somehow gotten to him first, instead of that brainless Max Stephan, he would have done a much better job. He explained to Rintelin that he would have taken Krug to a farm, improved his English, and taught him Spanish. He would have had Krug grow a mustache. Then, with built-up shoes, travelling by way of South America, Krug would certainly make it back. With Stephan it was questionable. Unfortunately for Donay, the weakest link in the whole episode, so far, was Rintelin. Donay's trust in him was totally misplaced.

As they left Donay's, Krug must have felt reasonably smug. His host for the day, as irritating as he was, had helped him acquire $40, but more than that, there was even the chance that the boastful Donay, in his cluttered little store, might even be able to get news of Camp W back to Germany. So while Stephan's personality was wearing thin, the man was nevertheless useful.

Driving away from Donay's, Stephan suggested one more stop; one that would complete the "everything" he had promised Krug he would help him catch up on. He suggested they visit a prostitute. It may have sounded like a pretty good idea to Krug and he may not have needed much arm twisting. After all, he was young and had been in prison for a year and a half. It was, therefore, not an unusual place to go and Canadian police frequently picked up escapees in Canadian whorehouses. To add a touch of humor to their reports they would sometimes indicate if the escapee had been recaptured before or after completion of his mission.

Anyway, Stephan drove to 54 Duffield Street, the "rooming house" of Mrs. Alvina Ludlow. She was a widow of some two

LUDLOW HOUSE
Alvina Ludlow's "house," Stephan's and Krug's last stop on April 18, 1942. FBI photo.

years who operated an establishment of 11 rooms. Stephan, who was well acquainted with Ludlow and her prostitutes, would sit this one out; after all, it was really a birthday present. He told Mrs. Ludlow that he was seeking some company for his friend. She said she had one vacant room but would have to call someone over. She called Mrs. "Peggy" Merrifield who, though reluctant, was finally persuaded to take the "engagement." She was temporarily and recently separated from her husband, Gaylord, whom she had married in 1920, the year Krug was born. She arrived by taxi in 20 minutes. By then, any thoughts of catching the 4 P.M. train were long forgotten.

There were two versions of what happened next. Mrs. Ludlow claimed that Peggy said that the party, Krug, didn't like her and wouldn't even talk to her, much less anything else. That could be the true version.

Peggy, of course, not wishing to end her career with any sort of a public admission like that, (Lets face it, Krug hadn't seen a woman in over a year) claimed to have completed her end of the bargain. She added that she asked Krug his name and couldn't quite make out the answer, but it was something about Milwaukee.

In any event, they were only in the room a few minutes and in everyone's version Krug gave her $3 which had previously been given to him by Stephan. Stephan also paid the small fee for the room and gave Peggy 60 cents on the way out for taxi fare.

The pair headed back to the restaurant with Krug undoubtedly thinking that in the unlikely event that he ever again would want a procurer in Detroit, he would find someone other than Max Stephan to guide him. They arrived at the restaurant at about 6 P.M.

Meanwhile Dietrich Rintelin, Donay's clerk, knew that he had a job to do. He had been under suspicion by the Enemy Alien Board, a wartime office that had authority to deal with persons linked to our enemies. Actually, Donay once put up bond for his release from detention. Rintelin had been picked up by the FBI just after Pearl Harbor and had been held for a short time while undoubtedly being reminded of his duty as a patriotic citizen. After his release he went back to work for Donay and there is little doubt that his role in life, insofar as the FBI was concerned, was to report on activities at the Europe Importing Company. He was listed with the FBI as confidential informant T-1. To add fuel to the matter, there was "bad blood" between Stephan and Rintelin.

At precisely 6:03 P.M. Rintelin fulfilled his responsibility to the FBI, by calling them and reporting the events of an hour or so earlier. The FBI then knew that Max Stephan was being seen around town with an escaped POW. For whatever reasons they had, the FBI did not make an arrest for another 30 hours. That fact did not even come out at Stephan's trial. It was revealed almost a year later at Donay's trial.

Back at the restaurant Krug was directed to one of the high-sided booths near the front. Mrs. Erna Schwartz, who had worked for Stephan for about five years, came over to serve him. She was an alien, of German descent, and born in Poland. She served Krug a supper of smoked pork loin and sauerkraut and he paid her the regular price of 52 cents. Through conversation, she was beginning to understand who and what Krug was. The same was true of Miss Christina Klein, the cook. She was also an alien, was of German descent, and had been born in Yugoslavia.

Krug had apparently recovered from the afternoon orgy and ordered some of Stephan's good beer to accompany the meal. While Krug was eating, two customers, well known to Max, entered the restaurant. They were Karl and Eva Erhardt and they had come in to see Max. The young couple had been married a week earlier and had held their reception in the back room. They were back on this particular evening to pay the balance of their bill. Karl would be in the Air Force in a few weeks. The couple went to the bar for a beer and Max, seeing his newlywed friends, came over. They chatted and Stephan indicated his "friend from Milwaukee" who, he suggested, they join. Meanwhile, word was spreading among the employes and few doubted who Krug was.

The Erhardts sat with Krug but few words were exchanged. Stephan was considering what he would do with Krug for the night. Earlier, before she knew his true identity, Erna Schwartz had offered to let him stay in the spare room in her home in Centerline. She lived there with her husband and three children. Max ruled that out and would not even consider letting him stay in the quarters over the restaurant. He gave Erna instructions to send Krug to the Field Hotel, around the corner from the restaurant.

At 9 P.M. Stephan was bracing for the evening rush. The Erhardts were still sitting with Krug. Conversation was limited, but it was a good cover. He would be too conspicuous alone and, in the custom of a German restaurant, anyone might come in and sit with him. Mrs. Schwartz came over to Krug and asked him to go with her to the back door. Krug

FIELD HOTEL
The Field Hotel where Krug stayed on the night of April 18, 1942. FBI photo.

accompanied her and she told him how he could go out the back way, through the alley, and into the Field Hotel. She told him to register as John Miller and to return to the restaurant at 8 o'clock the next morning, per Stephan's instructions.

Krug did as he was told and was waited on at the hotel by Walter J. Emerick, the desk clerk. Krug signed the registration card but had misunderstood the instructions. Mrs. Schwartz had given him the instructions in German. The name she told him to use, in German, was *Hans Müller.* Krug did not understand that he was supposed to translate that into John Miller.

He obediently registered as *Hans Müller*, complete with the German umlaut, the two dots, over the "u".

He further aroused suspicion when he failed to readily understand the request for $1.50 in advance. Emerick may have said something like, "that'll be a buck, fifty." This whole scene was witnessed by Chief Quartermaster (U.S. Navy) Merritt Barnes who was a resident of the Field Hotel and was, at the time, passing the time by talking with Emerick.

At about 11 P.M. on Saturday night, with Krug safely tucked into bed, Max's restaurant was visited by one of its more distinguished regular customers. He was William J. Nagel, a former postmaster of Detroit, who lived a few blocks away. Nagel was 68 years old at the time and had served as Detroit's postmaster from 1913 to 1922. In fact, the Postmaster General was said to have rated him as one of the country's top postmasters. He was a widower and lived with his daughter. His parents had come from Germany and he had been born in Detroit where he had attended high school and college. His appearance was impressive; six feet and one inch tall, 180 pounds, blue eyes, dark complexion, and bald with a gray fringe. He stopped by at least two or three times a week for one or two beers, which he customarily nursed very slowly. Frequently, as on this night, he would have a limburger cheese sandwich. Although he was a regular at the restaurant, he was not a close friend or crony of Stephan's, nor was he in any way involved in any of the German organizations that met there.

World War I had almost interrupted Nagel's career as postmaster until Postmaster General Burleson won a tug-of-war with the Army and he continued in his job. He had three brothers who had served in World War I in the American Army in France, one of whom had been killed and was buried there. In 1942 Nagel was still an active Democrat.

If in the arena of the political appointee, highly placed friends are a necessity, Nagel did not lack for them. He was a good friend of Frank Murphy, a man who had been Governor of Michigan and later, U.S. Attorney General. In 1942, Murphy was a U.S. Supreme Court Justice, having been appointed by Roosevelt two years earlier.

In respect to what happened next in the restaurant, there are two versions, Stephan's and Nagel's. Nagel's version can be given quite briefly. He maintained that there was never any mention of Krug in any conversation they might have had and that he had no knowledge of anything that was going on.

Stephan told a different story. He said that he told Nagel all about Krug and received counsel in return. According to Stephan, Nagel said, "Max, I would have done the same thing." Stephan further quoted Nagel as adding, "This is a prisoner of war, for him the war is over, it will only be a couple of days and he will be caught without you reporting him. His picture will be all over the United States." Stephan even claimed that Nagel offered to drive Krug to Chicago in his car, if he had the time, which he didn't, the story went. Stephan also claimed that Nagel suggested the bus instead of the train and contributed $3 for the fare. Both agreed that Nagel left the restaurant at about midnight.

Finally, the last customer gone, Stephan went through the evening ritual of locking up. Walter Emerick, the hotel clerk, had just gone off duty and was passing by. He tapped on the window to get Stephan's attention and the two talked briefly. He told Stephan that he thought he had taken in an escaped German. Stephan said, "Maybe so, you can't tell." Emerick wanted to bring him over in the morning so that Stephan could meet him. That was completely unnecessary, of course, and Stephan told Emerick not to bother. Whatever Emerick's suspicions were, somehow he did not feel motivated to call the FBI or the police.

By then Krug was fast asleep in the hotel. He must have dozed off knowing that he had spent a truly memorable birthday. It was certainly one that he could tell his grandchildren about ("*Ach so, mein kinder*") if he lived through this damnable war and had any. Of course, he would have to omit a few details. In fact, fifteen years later he would retell the story for the German magazine *Stern*. Understandably, he sanitized it and left out the part about the visit to Mrs. Ludlow's.

On the next day, Sunday, April 19, Krug appeared, bright and early at the appointed hour, 8 A.M. Stephan was ready

GREYHOUND STATION

Greyhound Bus Station in Detroit where Stephan put Krug on the bus for Chicago, Sunday, April 19, 1942. FBI photo.

and the pair did not delay. By now it appeared that Stephan was becoming increasingly concerned about his deep involvement in the whole matter. The pair immediately got into the car and went downtown. First they stopped at a barbeque restaurant and ordered chicken dinners, though Max had no appetite and left his on the plate. Then they went to the Greyhound Bus station at Grand River and Washington and Max bought a ticket to Chicago for Krug. One thing was plain, Max had invested a great deal of money in his new friend. They waited a short while and when it was time, Max helped Krug find the right bus. When he saw his weekend guest off, he completed what would be the final "overt" act in the list of charges against him.

The next day the bus driver, Joseph O'Malley would be

shown Krug's photo but would be unable to make a match between it and anyone who had boarded his bus. Krug's photo trick had worked and for a while the FBI could not say with certainty that Krug had left the city.

The Detroit experience had been a strange one for Krug and he could only wonder if Chicago would be the same. It was an odd group that he had met. On one hand he had accomplished much; he now had more money, and he may have passed word of Camp W and Müller back to Germany. On the other hand Stephan had been unbelievably haphazard he thought, particularly in the way he had put him up for the night. Stephan's views of world affairs had been ludicrous. The man believed that peace would be arranged between the U.S. and Germany, after Germany had attained peace in Europe. Krug thought that Stephan felt he would be the recipient of great honor once that occurred.[10] Was it possible that he thought of himself as, God forbid, the future *Gaulieter* of Detroit?

After seeing Krug off, Max drove back to the restaurant. At about 11 A.M. he called Mrs. Bertelmann. Her husband, who was still completely unaware of what had happened, answered and called to her, saying, "It is for you, it is Max Stephan."

Stephan said to her, "Well, he is gone." Then he did a curious thing. They were both deeply involved at that point but he saw fit to perform a minor bit of blackmail. He insisted that she help wait on tables at the meeting of the Schwaben Society that evening. She objected saying that she had never done that type of work before. She said she didn't have an apron, a poor reason, and she made other excuses. Stephan was insistent. Sarcastically he said, "Well, you have to do something, I can't get help. Don't forget, your country is at war." With that, Mrs. Bertelmann agreed to help.

She arrived at the restaurant late in the afternoon. As she was preparing for work, Mrs. Erna Schwartz followed her to the ladies room. Mrs. Schwartz said, "Well, he is gone." They were the same words spoken by Max, and Mrs. Bertelmann had little doubt that all the employes knew who Krug was.

At 6 P.M. the meeting of the Schwaben Society was ready to begin. This was the friendly little gathering that Krug had declined to attend. The meeting started in the usual manner, with the singing of God Bless America. But for the hard core there was a reason for the festivities to be extra special this evening. It was the eve of the 20th of April, Adolph Hitler's 53rd birthday, and for some the party was planned to go on far into the night. Although Max didn't know it, he had seen his last day of freedom.

At midnight there were twenty celebrants left in the restaurant, the remnants of the Schwaben Society meeting. The *Fuhrer's* birthday party (happy birthday, dear Adolph?) was just getting into full swing when a small, unsmiling group entered the back room and requested that everyone avail themselves of the waiting transportation and accompany them to FBI headquarters.

Chapter 7

A Charge of Treason

In 1942 the Detroit FBI office was headed by John S. Bugas who was later to leave the FBI and become a Vice President of Ford Motor Company. In fact, Bugas was to become a trusted ally to Henry Ford II. Bugas stood by young Henry at a critical time, when it was necessary to fire Bennett, the strong-arm union buster originally hired by young Henry's grandfather.

Bugas was six days short of his 34th birthday when he led his men into Stephan's restaurant on the night of April 19, 1942. He had graduated from the University of Wyoming in 1934 and had served the FBI in Washington, Los Angeles, Omaha, Alaska, and Birmingham, before Detroit. The Detroit assignment had begun in 1938.

John Bugas and his wife lived at the Whittier Hotel, just off Jefferson Avenue on the Detroit River, and not far from Stephan's restaurant. John Bugas had visited the restaurant on a number of occasions, had tasted Stephan's famous German beer, and knew Max on sight.

FBI records had, for some time, contained information relating to the pro-German and pro-Nazi activities in the U.S. Prior to the U.S. entry into the war the FBI had simply maintained surveillance, watched, waited, and collected information. The FBI's major compilation at the time was the so-called National Security Index, in effect a *Who's Who* of potential subversives. The name of Max Stephan was contained in the document. When the U.S. entered the war, surveillance was increased on those listed in the Index. Raids were occasionally conducted, netting caches of arms and Nazi flags. Stephan was still perfectly within the law, however, with his meetings of the Schwaben and Steuben Societies.

When Krug escaped and patrol activity was increased, the FBI also increased their own surveillance. Then on Saturday, April 18th, at 6:03 P.M., they received the tip from informant T-1, Dietrich Rintelin, and had the information that Stephan was escorting an escapee around the city. There is little in the way of factual information to tell us what the FBI did for the next 30 hours. Their records make no mention of it. Possibly they increased their surveillance of Stephan, in hopes of catching Krug. If that was the case, then it is also true that Krug slipped through their net. If their plan was to follow Krug and pick up more subversives, it did not work. There is no indication that Krug was followed. The best guess is that Rintelin's message was misplaced, or because of the weekend, just didn't get to the right people in time.

In any event, at midnight on Sunday, April 19, when the FBI entered the restaurant, the party came to a sudden and gloomy end. The entire group, including Max and Mrs. Bertelmann, were taken to FBI headquarters for questioning. Everyone was released except Max Stephan. John Bugas took a lengthy statement from him in which he admitted everything in full detail. Before taking the statement, Bugas advised him that he was very possibly in most serious trouble and that anything he said might be used against him. Stephan put the whole saga into the statement, even such details as telling Krug to go downtown and look at the buildings for awhile. The statement also included Stephan's version of the encounter with William Nagel in the restaurant on Saturday night. It was a detailed admission of the entire episode and when it was completed, Stephan signed his name at the bottom.

There is no question that Stephan knew that he had no chance of denying anything and that his only chance to salvage anything was to cooperate fully and hope for leniency on that basis. After all, he had escorted Krug so openly that the government would have no trouble finding good witnesses.

Stephan was held in the Wayne County Jail with an entire cell block to himself.

The story was not made public on Monday, possibly because the questioning was still in progress. However, on Tuesday, April 21, the news was printed and people first read the story in the Detroit Free Press, the morning paper. Reporters were granted almost unlimited access to Stephan. Their stories were illustrated with pictures of the pudgy, round faced Stephan, coatless, but wearing a vest over his shirt and tie. About the only person who could not talk to him was his wife, Agnes.

Reflecting on his arrest he said to reporters, "I wonder how the FBI found out about this. I must have talked too much." He was partly right, but he did not know about Rintelin.

For Detroit, the story was a big one. After all, now the war that everyone thought was so far away, had moved right into the city. For many Detroiters it would be the closest they would ever come to the enemy. The papers hit hard on the aspects of the case that would tend to infuriate people, and Stephan made the job quite easy.

He started talking cooperatively enough, telling all about Krug and his plans to go to Mexico, South America, and then to Spain. Meanwhile Krug read of his own plans as he travelled.

Stephan spoke of his call from Mrs. Bertelmann. He gave a full account of Krug, obviously as proud of him as he might be of his own son. Krug apparently told the story of the crash landing off the coast of England and from that Stephan concluded, probably correctly, that Krug possessed above average flying skill. Stephan passed his impressions on to the press, saying that Krug was a good flier. It seemed as though Stephan enjoyed the spotlight. He said that Krug loved to fly and wanted to get a "stick" in his hands again—a quote with serious implications. He told of the "tommy" being shot down by Krug's crew.

Stephan said he told Krug that he didn't have a chance. Krug, he said, was a smart boy though, and while most could not do it, he would. Stephan even spoke of how Krug had predicted a German victory in the fall and wanted to get back while the war was still on. He told of how smart Krug had been to have remembered Mrs. Bertelmann's address.

As for himself, he said he had only done what any American would have done in Germany in a similar, but reversed, situation. Krug was, as he put it, "a home country fellow." He asked if he would do it again and he said he "guessed he would," but that was a "have you stopped beating your wife" type question, anyway. Asked about his loyalty to the U.S., he said he never thought we would fight Germany.

At times he became more melancholy and disjointed. He said, "I helped a German officer escape and I won't squeal on him, so what? Well they say that I am a terrible criminal and they sentence me to jail. I know my restaurant business is ruined, now they are taking away my citizenship. What difference does it make? No matter what they do to me I can always get along . . . Here we have too much of everything. I sat down to a big chicken dinner Sunday morning when I was seeing Krug off for Chicago. He enjoyed it immensely. I could not eat. Hunger is the best cook. To be hungry like Krug is to enjoy your food." It is not clear what all that meant, except possibly that Max Stephan was finally realizing that he was in big, big trouble.

He told of letting the Red Cross Ladies use the restaurant but was called to task by a reporter, "Weren't those the same Red Cross Ladies who sent packages to German prisoners in Canada?'"

In an occasional show of confidence he said, "I won't be in jail long." He expressed concern for his supply of cigars which he chain smoked. He described himself, perhaps aptly, as, "a man who takes the middle way."

For all practical purposes the trial had been held during this period of questioning by reporters. All that was left was some brief formality in the courtroom.

Initially he was charged with concealing and harboring an alien. According to U.S. District Attorney John C. Lehr that was the same charge that was used in peacetime against a citizen who had helped an alien enter the country illegally. The penalty for that was a maximum of five years in jail,

$2,000, or both. As far as Detroit was concerned, the likes of Max Stephan deserved much more.

On April 22, the Wednesday after Krug's departure, the restaurant license was revoked. That was the day that a Detroit Times headline said;

"NAZI FLIER ELUDES FBI"

Another headline said;

"KRUG STILL AT LARGE"

His description was in all the papers and read;

> "This is Krug: 21 years old,
> although looks older
> 5 ft., 8½ in., 157 pounds
> brown hair, brown eyes,
> straight nose, round chin,
> very erect walk,
> decided German accent."

His FBI poster photo and the newspaper pictures of him were the old ones with the glasses.

Also on April 22nd a name out of Stephan's past reappeared. It was Mrs. Sanger, the female half of the couple who had helped the Stephan's falsify their residency back in 1929. Mr. Sanger was dead and Mrs. Sanger was making her home in the Windsor house that they had built when they knew the Stephans. She had just returned from California and discovered that her boathouse had been broken into. She claimed that the key to her motorboat was gone, also. There were implications that the break in report was a cover-up in a larger plot and that Krug had been transported across the river.

During that same period, just following the arrest, the name of former Postmaster William Nagel came up. He was implicated to the degree that in Stephan's version he had knowledge of Krug on Saturday night. Stephan was later to claim that shortly after his arrest Nagel called Agnes and told her to meet him some place where they would not be recognized together. At that alleged meeting Nagel was supposed to have said that

WANTED

PRISONER OF WAR - ESCAPED GERMAN AVIATOR

Photo taken within past year.

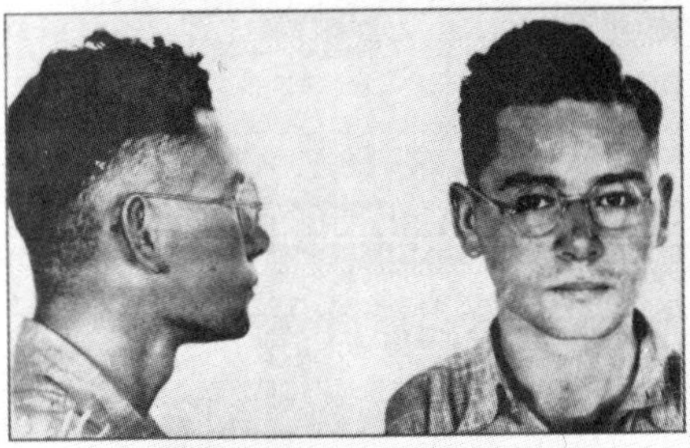

PETER KRUG, alias Muller

Peter Krug, alias Peter Muller, a German aviator, escaped from the Concentration Camp at Bowmanville, Ontario, Canada, before dawn on April 16, 1942. He was being held as a prisoner of war. After effecting his escape, he was able to reach Detroit, Michigan, on April 18, 1942, by rowing a boat across the Detroit River. On April 19, 1942, he departed from Detroit, Michigan, via bus, ostensibly for Chicago, Illinois, to contact another individual, after which he planned on returning to Germany via South America.

DESCRIPTION

Age:	21	Nose:	Straight
Height:	5' 8½"	Chin:	Round
Weight:	157 pounds	Build:	Medium
Complexion:	Fair - tanned	Carriage:	Very erect, military
Eyes:	Brown; possibly wearing horn-rimmed glasses	Language:	Speaks German, practically no English
Hair:	Long, wavy	Clothes:	Possibly wearing dirty coveralls over dark blue dress suit and grey cap.
Marks:	Full mole on left shoulder blade.		

If you are in possession of any information concerning the whereabouts of Peter Krug, alias Muller, communicate immediately in person or by telephone or telegraph "collect" to the undersigned or to the nearest office of the Federal Bureau of Investigation, U. S. Department of Justice, the local address and telephone numbers of which are set forth on the reverse side of this notice.

JOHN EDGAR HOOVER, DIRECTOR
FEDERAL BUREAU OF INVESTIGATION
UNITED STATES DEPARTMENT OF JUSTICE
WASHINGTON, D. C.
TELEPHONE, NATIONAL 7117

April 22, 1942

WANTED

FBI poster of Peter Krug. The photograph is the one taken a year earlier by the Canadians and Krug is wearing borrowed glasses. There is no basis for the "Peter Muller" except that Krug registered as "Hans Müller" at the Field Hotel in Detroit. FBI photo.

Stephan had talked too much and that he, Nagel, could do more for Max if his name was left out of the case entirely. He was supposed to have claimed that by leaving him out he could work quietly in the background, using his considerable influence, to help Stephan. Nagel confirmed that he had conversations with Mrs. Stephan but denied ever making such statements. He was not called as a witness at the trial, but then, in his version there was no reason why he should have been.

By April 22nd Mrs. Bertelmann was also in custody. She was held on the same charge as Stephan, but also had a second charge against her; that of possessing a short wave radio of a type that, as an alien, she was supposed to have either turned in or registered.

Mr. Bertelmann was also questioned. However, he said that he was at work and knew nothing about what his wife had done. He offered to cooperate in every way with the FBI. That was certainly a wise move for anyone whose home seemed to be a way station on an underground railway. Also on the 22nd, Lehr, the U.S. District Attorney, asked for a charge of treason against Stephan. He did not have the authority to make that charge on his own. The decision would have to come down from U.S. Attorney General Francis Biddle and he would not decide immediately.

The papers gave us a bit of trivia on April 24 when they told us that Adolph Hitler of Moscow, Michigan joined the U.S. Army.

Then to everyone's relief, the May 2 headline read;

"KRUG CAUGHT IN TEXAS"

He had been recaptured the previous day in San Antonio after having made an epic journey as a fugitive. To protect the people who had helped him, he told a fabricated tale of his trip which was generally accepted in spite of a few suspicious points. The story of his travels would not become general knowledge until fifteen years later, in the German magazine, *Stern*. At that time the story was somewhat embellished by a creative writer.

Krug had arrived in Chicago on Sunday, April 19 and contacted one of his memorized names. He was passed on to several others and he recognized that he was in the hands of much different types of people than in Detroit. These were subversives with a national network. Krug felt that they were extremely businesslike. At first the poor likeness in the newspaper pictures actually hurt him. They did not believe who he was. They thought he was an FBI agent and finally, using his officer's epaulet and his powers of persuasion he was able to convince them. They took notes while he told them of Canada and the shooting of Müller.

Finally, after several days, they outfitted him in a suit of clothes, including one of those garish American neckties he had seen, along with a suitcase and some extra clothing. They gave him $100 in twenties and prepared to send him on his way. They were not able to provide him with false papers, and for those, they had him memorize an address in Philadelphia where he would go next.

On Thursday, April 23, a lady in the group took him to the bus station. He later recalled riding eastward through Illinois, Indiana, Ohio, and Pennsylvania. What romantic names ("*Was für romantische namen*"), he thought, and the countryside, my God, it was a big country. The lights were on in the cities, there was more food than he had seen in a long time, and there were cars on the road. Even though Americans thought they were making sacrifices, to Krug it didn't even look like wartime.[10]

Arriving in Philadelphia on April 24, he went straight to the address he had been given in Chicago. As he walked up to the house a lady across the street put her head out of the window and shouted, "If you want that damned Nazi, the police arrested him yesterday." He wished he could disappear, but he managed to reply with something and walked away as quickly as possible. He thought surely the place must have been watched and took two trolleys in rapid succession, then a taxi to the railway station. He did not feel that he had satisfactory enough papers to get to Mexico and decided to go to New York to an address he had memorized back in Bowmanville.

He arrived in New York that same day and took a taxi to the

street he had memorized. Although he already knew of Stephan's arrest, while riding in the taxi he read a full account of Stephan in a paper he had picked up. The article included a large picture of Stephan laughing, standing between two policeman. Donay was mentioned. There were pictures of the restaurant, everything. Krug was disturbed and alarmed.

Leaving the taxi he walked to the house number and introduced himself. The man and wife were sympathetic toward him and let him stay for the weekend. They had no connection with the underground and could not possibly help him with false papers. Some friends of his host and hostess dropped by and offered to let him stay on their farm for six months, until the search died down. However, after reading about Stephan he was concerned about anyone who might help him, and he decided to move on.[10]

On Monday, April 27 he left for Pittsburgh, the first leg of his journey to Mexico. He would still be Jean Etté, but now he would be travelling to Little Rock, Arkansas to a Free French training camp. On the bus to Pittsburgh he conversed with a 16 year old girl who apparently was very impressed with the stories the young "Frenchman" told. She invited him to go home with her, and though the temptation was great, he declined. Continuing on, he went to Cincinnati, Louisville, and Nashville, where he stayed overnight in a hotel. The next morning at breakfast he picked up a newspaper that was left on the table by the previous customer. A map labelled "Defense Map of America" fell out. It was something that was issued by the Greyhound Bus Company, not too wisely perhaps, and showed the location of many major military bases in the U.S. He felt that he had made a significant find and put the map among his possessions, hopefully to take back to Germany. He then bought a ticket to Dallas, which was planned as the second to the last stop on his way to Mexico.

On that leg of the trip he was once again met by temptation, so his story goes. When the bus stopped in Memphis a girl named Margaret sat down beside him. She was 18 and had long blond hair. At 18 she was much more sophisticated than Dorothy. He entertained her with his stories and the two became friends during the trip. She was on her way to see her uncle who had "the finest ranch in Texas." Once again he was invited to stay there and again fought temptation and turned down the offer. When the bus stopped in Dallas he met the uncle who was sitting in a tremendous Cadillac, looking, he thought, like a General Motors advertisement. Sadly, he watched them ride off.[10]

On the morning of May 1 he arrived in San Antonio. He planned to get a hotel room, rest, get some supplies, and then the next day make the final dash to Laredo where he would swim the Rio Grande River and be in Mexico. That country was still neutral and he would go to the German Embassy in Mexico City where he would be as good as home. But he wasn't there yet. In San Antonio he looked for a hotel. Spotting a large, clean looking one he started to enter and stopped in his tracks. It was filled with U.S. Air Force officers. Searching again he found a small, back street hotel, the Nueces. The newspapers would repeatedly make an error in phonetics and refer to it as the "New Aces" Hotel. He asked for a single room. The proprietor, an overweight blond woman, said, "We only have double rooms." He thought she smiled rather oddly. Not wishing to arouse suspicion, which he probably already had, he took the room. "Ten dollars," she said. He was totally surprised and could not believe that a room in this fleabag hotel would be ten dollars. Still not wanting to arouse suspicion, he paid the money. It was obvious that he had gone to a hotel that did more than rent rooms.[10]

He put his belongings in his room and went out to buy supplies for the rest of his trip. First he bought some canned food and candy. Then he bought some local-style clothes. He felt out of place in the Chicago suit that he was still wearing. Last, for $13.50 he bought a .25 caliber Colt automatic pistol and for another $1.50, some ammunition for it. He turned down a .44 caliber British Bulldog revolver because of his contempt for the British.

At 10 P.M. that evening he went back to the hotel, into the lobby, past the proprietor, and upstairs to his room. At some point he marked his route on the Greyhound "Defense Map."

Unfortunately for him, both his conduct and his accent had attracted suspicion. The FBI had passed out his wanted poster at most hotels, including the Nueces. When the blond woman heard his accent she became suspicious, called the FBI, and told them about the strange guest that had registered. This time Krug was not dealing with Walter Emerick at the Field Hotel in Detroit. Shortly after 11 P.M. a team of four men were outside of room 307. They were FBI agent Jack O. Parker, another FBI agent, and Sergeant Robinson and Officer Leichman of the San Antonio police. Krug was awakened and called the desk to say that he was being disturbed. The proprietor came up and verified that the persons in the hall were not robbers. With guns drawn, they entered. Krug, in pajamas, was asked to identify himself and he showed them the false letters in which he was Jean Etté. Then Sergeant Robinson found the gun under a hat on the dresser. A further search uncovered the map in the suitcase. Certainly it was a map that was available to the public but it was particularly suspicious because of the way the route was drawn on it. The epaulets were found. Where did he come from, where was he going, and who was he, they thought? Was he, indeed, Peter Krug?

Krug was asked to get dressed and he put on his new clothes; khaki pants, a yellow short sleeved shirt, and heavy black shoes. Meanwhile, his belongings were collected. So far, Krug had not admitted who he really was. They only knew that they had a "wanted" poster in their office and a very suspicious character on their hands. He was suspicious indeed, with the accent, the gun, the curiously marked map, the supplies, and the strange papers.

In the car Krug tried to swallow an address and kick a note under the seat, which added to suspicions. At headquarters the questioning proceeded. Finally at 2:30 A.M. on May 2nd, Peter Krug admitted who he was. He was placed in the San Antonio Jail and became something of a celebrity there. He arrogantly protested being fingerprinted like a common criminal. Prominent citizens stopped by to see him and local reporters went on a feeding frenzy. He was quoted at length, particularly in regard to his feelings about Americans. "The majority," he was quoted, "are utterly stupid." He explained how easily people had accepted his thick accent and his forged papers, which he claimed to have used eight times. When told that he had done good to get as far as he had, he was quoted as saying, "everything we do is good."

He had vastly improved his knowledge of colloquial English in his travels and could interject words like "sure." Once when questioned in German he said, "If you can't speak better German than that, I'd rather talk in English."

Actually, after he disclosed his identity, there was still some question as to whether he should be held for espionage. It was a serious charge, one that could bring a death sentence. While the U.S. probably would not have pressed the matter, the English stepped in and intervened. They advised the U.S. that Krug was a prisoner of war and "the property and guest of His Majesty the King." To be saved by the British that way, left a lasting impression on him.[10] Four FBI agents took him north to the border and handed him over to Canadian authorities.

It had been a typical recapture. In the German memoirs of the escapes, American police were generally ridiculed. In one of their stories a small town *Inspektor* bemoaned his fate and wished for an assignment in Chicago where he might have a shoot-out with Al Capone and his gang. The prisoners didn't really understand America. Generally, fugitives were caught after being turned in by alert clerks or waitresses who had heard or read the escapee's description. In one instance a waitress at a lunch counter called the police. It was usually as simple as that.

Back in Bowmanville Krug was given the customary 28 days in close confinement. Later he would regale his envious comrades with stories and graphic descriptions of the wonderful whorehouses he had visited in the U.S. One of the listeners was a *Luftwaffe* pilot by the name of Frederick von Goetz who, after being returned to Germany at the end of the war, later emigrated to Canada and settled in Toronto.

Krug had one pleasant surprise waiting for him upon his return to camp. A letter from his parents informed him that he had been promoted to *Oberleutnant*, comparable to a First

Lieutenant. It would be a short time before the Canadian government would receive official notification through the Swiss authorities. People would say that he had been promoted as a reward for his brilliant escape but he would refute that, claiming that it took at least two months for a promotion to come through from Germany. In any event, there was no doubt that he was warmly congratulated by Colonel Hefele, the senior prisoner-officer who was later replaced by U-boat commander Otto Kretschmar.

When Krug returned to Bowmanville, two other prisoners were missing; "Doc" Wagner, and Pfundtner, the former exchange student. It was about then that the "top escapers" were to be sent to the new "escape proof" prison at Gravenhurst Barracks. Krug was soon sent there along with Steinhilper, the recaptured Wagner and Pfundtner, and others.

The U.S. Government was building its case against Max Stephan simultaneously with Krug's return to Canada. As the investigation proceeded, John Bugas was to pursue a creative course of action. It started when FBI agents began to understand what made Krug tick, in the early stages of the investigation. He was asked to view various individuals that were involved and was told that he might regard it as his duty to clear the innocent and identify the guilty. The agents immediately recognized that this appealed to Krug. He seemed to be controlling American justice. It was obvious that he was an egotist of the first order and to make matters worse or better, depending on whose side you're on, his officer training had apparently reinforced that character trait and dictated that he be in control of any and all situations that he was a part of. Under the rules of the Geneva Convention a prisoner could never be forced to testify against the people who had helped him, so Krug, if he was to play a part in events, would have to do so voluntarily.

In government circles it was felt that in this landmark case it would be of great help to the prosecution if the beneficiary of the treasonous act, Krug, gave testimony at the trial. Gradually, the FBI began to realize that there was a chance that they could persuade Krug to volunteer to do just that. They talked to him on the basis that he was only being asked to tell the truth. They implied that in doing so, Krug, the *Luftwaffe*, and indeed the entire German officer caste, would be held in high esteem throughout the world. Certainly, it was hinted, even enemies would look with admiration upon so forthright a person. As Bugas explained it, the system from which he came would be glorified and all "Nazi-dom" would be exalted. That was the premise, even though Bugas probably had difficulty keeping a straight face.

They visited Krug frequently to reinforce the premise. When they found that he liked candy they would bring a small bag with them. Another agent, who was well versed in German, told Krug that he would like some German lessons. Krug volunteered and this further appealed to his ego, to be teaching an agent of the FBI. The agent later showed marked improvement which Krug attributed to his teaching.

When it was agreed that Krug would testify, he asked for a German-English dictionary. One was given to him and he promptly wrote on the flyleaf, "A gift from my very good friends of the FBI this 17th day of June at Windsor, Ontario, Canada.

Over and above the matter of his giant ego, that the FBI successfully played upon, Krug did have some personal thoughts on the matter. He knew that Stephan was a victim of his own stupidity and would be convicted. He may have even felt that he could show that the crime was stupidity, rather than treason. Certainly he felt guilt and responsibility and may have thought that he could prevent a death sentence by verifying that he had met Stephan through Mrs. Bertelmann and that Stephan was not an underground agent. He felt even more concern for Mrs. Bertelmann and did indeed want to verify that she was not a part of any underground network. He could truthfully say that he had gone to her without knowing if she would help. He felt a responsibility to do those things, and discussed it with his fellow officers. It was agreed that he would testify.

In addition, he would tell a fabricated story of the rest of his travels so that, he felt, the FBI might not pursue that subject any further. But there was another reason, too. He and all the prisoners felt that it was valuable to learn as much as possible about America. That sort of thing would be useful in future escapes.

So it came down to a combination of factors that encouraged him to testify, a convincing story by the FBI and some personal rationalizations.

We know that full military rank and authority prevailed among the prisoners and it is difficult to understand that cooler heads, among his peers and superiors, did not prevail and prevent him from testifying. Part of the reason for that could have been a lack of knowledge about the American legal system. Krug may have expected to simply tell his story before a panel of judges. In any event, once he told Bugas he would testify, he became the cornerstone of the Government's case. John Bugas did not consider him to be particularly bright.

Naturally there had been no contact between Stephan and Krug and Stephan would never understand why Krug came back.

The war news was still not encouraging. On May 6, Corregidor, the last outpost in the Philippines, fell and the American captives followed their comrades from Bataan into the death cells. On May 23rd Mexico declared war on the Axis powers, having lost three ships to German torpedoes. Had Krug not been recaptured in San Antonio he probably would have had little trouble getting through Mexico while they were still neutral.

In Detroit, Mexico's entry into the war was not that important on that day. What was important on the 23rd was that the decision had been handed down by Attorney General Biddle. Stephan was to be charged with treason, punishable by a sentence of from five years in prison to death. Treason cases have never been every day events and there was little precedent for them. Stephan's particular form of the crime has also been referred to as "high" treason. In old English law that distinguished it from petit or petty treason which was the killing of a master by his slave or a husband by his wife.

It quickly built into a major case. Stephan commented, "I think it is to get into the newspapers so that other German people will not do things like that. But in my heart I do not feel I am guilty of treason."

At times the tide of the war could be seen to change, ever so slightly. On June 5, Cologne, the Stephan's old city received massive damage in an air raid. The RAF was retaliating for the raids on Britain. *Gaulieter* Grohe of Cologne had to take steps to stop looters.

On the other side of the world an event of far greater importance was in the making. It was the Battle of Midway, which ended on June 6, with the Japanese in full retreat. The battle was a classic in its interplay of strategy, wits, guts, and luck. The Japanese advanced on Midway Island, a tiny atoll, 1,200 miles northwest of Hawaii, with battleships, troop carriers, and four aircraft carriers, the Kaga, the Akagi, the Siryu, and the Hiryu. We had three aircraft carriers to oppose them, the Hornet, the Enterprise, and the Yorktown which was not completely repaired from an earlier battle in the Coral Sea.

The essence of the battle was that the Japanese carrier commanders waffled in deciding whether to arm their planes with bombs, for Midway, or torpedoes, for the American fleet which they had not yet fully located. In the confusion, their carrier decks were stacked with both bombs and torpedoes, along with the gasoline for refueling. At that moment a wave of American planes attacked and all but the Hiryu immediately became raging infernos, sinking later that day. The Hiryu was hit the same day but did not sink until June 9.

There had been epic heroism in the American attack. Our pilots were inexperienced and our planes were woefully obsolete. We lost the carrier Yorktown, but the tally sheet was greatly in our favor. The Japanese suffered their first major defeat of the War, four carriers sunk in one battle, almost six months to the day after they had fired the opening shot at Pearl Harbor. They retreated with their invasion force and remaining ships and lost the offensive.

The Battle of Midway was notable in another respect, too. A new form of sea warfare had evolved. The role of the battleships, firing within sight of each other, had passed. Now the sea battle was between aircraft carriers that were never visible to each other.

On June 18 Stephan was indicted for treason before Federal Judge Edward J. Moinet. Krug, in a preview of things to come, had testified before the Federal Grand Jury that returned the indictment. The charge was that Max Stephan "Treasonably and traitorously adhered and gave aid and comfort to an enemy of the U.S." Thirteen overt acts were charged;

1. He went to Mrs. Bertelmann's house for the purpose of taking Krug under his protection.
2. He obtained money from Mrs. Bertelmann for Krug.
3. He escorted Krug from Mrs. Bertelmann's house.
4. He escorted Krug to the restaurant.
5. He provided food, clothing, and personal effects.
6. He made inquiries regarding train and bus schedules to Chicago.
7. He escorted Krug to Haller's Cafe and introduced him as one of Meier's boys.
8. He escorted Krug to the Progressive Club and bought drinks.
9. He escorted Krug to the business place of Theodore Donay and obtained money for Krug.
10. He took Krug to a disorderly house.
11. He took Krug back to his restaurant.
12. He directed and gave orders to register Krug as a guest at the Field Hotel.
13. He took Krug to the bus station at Washington and Grand River and bought a ticket to Chicago.

It was charged that the objective was to get Krug to Mexico, then South America, and then back to Germany to resume active duty in the German air force.

Since Mrs. Bertelmann was not a citizen she could not be charged with treason. After the trial she would be sent to Texas to a camp for enemy aliens.

Stephan's attorney, Vern C. Amberson, asked that Stephan be arraigned on Friday, June 19. Arraignment was completed before 74 year old federal Judge Arthur J. Tuttle of whom we will hear much more. It was two months since Stephan had put Krug on the bus. The trial was set to start on Monday, June 29 and a current quote from Stephan was, "I'm in a hell of a mess."

June 19 was also the day when "scarface" Theodore Donay was arrested and accused of aiding in Krug's escape. He scorned the arresting authorities, saying, "If this were Germany I would give you my card and challenge you to a duel." It was a widely quoted remark and it showed how out of touch he was with Germany. He complained that his bond, set at $50,000 was too high. Possibly he did not consider himself as worthy as von Werra.

Donay, when questioned by the FBI, disclaimed any knowledge of who Krug was. The FBI pursued the point more closely by asking Donay if he had informed the authorities of Krug's visit. Donay said that was absurd. Since he didn't know who Krug was, why would he have notified anyone, he said.

He was charged with "misprision" of treason. That meant aiding in the act of treason. Three overt acts were charged;

1. Knowledge that Stephan brought Krug to his place of business.
2. Knowledge that Stephan bought candy for Krug.
3. Giving $20 to Krug.

Donay may hold an unenviable place in American history as the only person ever charged with misprision of treason. The legal neophyte might ask the question; What is the difference between treason and aiding in treason? The government, in replying to this question pointed to the Constitutional requirement for two witnesses to the crime of treason, something they claimed was missing with Donay. That was not really true, since Rintelin and Stephan, not to mention Krug, were all witnesses. We can only assume that the Attorney General's office felt that one treason trial was enough. They may have felt that they had their main participant in Stephan and the others were of lesser importance. The government was mainly concerned with Donay's act of concealment, since on April 20 he had been asked about Krug and had denied seeing him.

Judge Moinet told Donay, "You are charged with unlawfully, knowingly, and treacherously concealing and that you did not disclose to President, Judge, or Governors, or any individual, the identity of Peter Krug, an enemy of the United States. Donay replied, "I am not guilty of being a traitor, your honor." By then the FBI was busy sifting through the two truckloads of documents they had carried away from the Europe Importing Company. Actually, Donay would have to wait for a while before he could be tried. Stephan would have to be convicted of treason, and the appeal process would have to be exhausted, before Donay could be convicted of helping him do it.

With Stephan's trial set for Monday, June 29, the preceding weekend was a time for stage setting. Krug was back in town for his voluntary appearance at the trial. He was resplendent in his *Luftwaffe* dress uniform, complete with the insignia of an *Oberleutnant.* His promotion had finally been recognized by the Canadian Government and the insignia of his new rank had been made for him by a Canadian jeweler. That the Canadians went to that much trouble, is certainly to their credit. It would have been easier if they had simply told Krug to borrow an insignia of rank from another *Oberleutnant.*

Krug was under heavy guard and was escorted by a Canadian Officer of equivalent rank, in accordance with the Geneva Convention. He carried the FBI's gift dictionary.

U.S. District Attorney Lehr was to prosecute the case in court, assisted by John W. Babcock who would do most of the questioning. Lehr discussed the prosecution's case in somedetail beforehand. He explained that under the Constitution, treason is divided into two parts;

ON THE WAY TO COURT

Krug being escorted to court by Canadian officer of equal rank. Krug is carrying the dictionary given to him by the FBI. (Reprinted with the permission of the Detroit Free Press.)

1. Levying war against the U.S., or
2. Adhering to the enemy, giving them aid and comfort.

The second of the two was to be the basis of the case, Lehr explained. He also explained that under the Constitution a conviction must come either from open confession in court or by two witnesses to the same overt act of treason. He went on further to explain that the technicalities centered around the question of whether or not Stephan's acts constituted a breach of allegiance and on his intent in committing them.

Stephan's attorney, Amberson, did not reveal any plans and in truth did not really have much of anything in the way of a viable defense. Indications from Amberson were that Stephan would disclaim responsibility, pleading ignorance of the law. In discussing the upcoming case Amberson described Stephan as a man who was motivated to help someone who was without friends; possibly the understatement of 1942 and certainly a thin defense against a serious charge.

Amberson, a World War I veteran, was certainly competent, but the Stephans had not found many attorneys willing to handle the case. Amberson had actually sought out the Stephans. An anonymous woman, who was later said to have been Amberson's secretary, had called Agnes and suggested him. He was acutely aware that he was being criticized for taking the case of an accused traitor. He knew that people had difficulty separating the lawyer from the client and he would make public statements several times, aimed at keeping the taint of Stephan off his hands.

As is frequently the case, he and the prosecutor, Lehr, were acquainted outside the courtroom. They sometimes rode the bus together to Monroe, south of Detroit, where Lehr lived and Amberson served in some official capacity. It is certainly possible that Lehr, aware that Stephan was having difficulty finding a lawyer, asked Amberson to step in.

In addition to Krug, the prosecution had a long list of witnesses lined up to testify. They included most of the key parties from the famous Saturday as well as FBI agents and Canadian Armed Forces personnel.

Chapter 8

The United States of America vs. Max Stephan

The judge who was to preside over the trial was the crusty, 74 year old Arthur J. Tuttle who had roots going back to the Revolutionary War. His great-great-grandfather was General Joseph Warren who had not just participated in the Revolution, but had directed some of the more important events. In 1764, at the age of 23, Joseph Warren began the practice of medicine in Boston. In 1765, when the Stamp Act was passed, he entered politics and soon became one of Massachusetts' leaders in the movement for independence. He was the man who sent Paul Revere on his famous ride on April 18, 1775. Three days after being appointed a Major General by the Massachusetts Provincial Assembly, he was killed fighting in the ranks at the battle of Bunker Hill. His body was buried at the battle site and later exhumed and identified by Paul Revere, who had done Warren's dental work.

A granddaughter of General Warren married a John J. Tuttle in New York State. They left there in 1836 to settle in south-central Michigan near the town of Leslie, just south of Lansing. Michigan was then opening up to settlement and many of the new arrivals were coming from New York State. Those settlers, if they were willing to make the sacrifices, could sell their New York farms for much more than the price of a Michigan homestead.

The Tuttles had three children, one of whom was named Ogden Valorous. Ogden, who remained in Leslie, married Elizabeth MacArthur and they had three children. One was Arthur J., born November 8, 1868.

Arthur J. Tuttle studied law at the University of Michigan and was admitted to the bar in 1895. He practiced law for awhile in the town of Leslie and became President of the People's Bank of Leslie. He moved his law practice to Lansing and then served as Prosecuting Attorney for Ingham County from 1899 to 1902. On March 11, 1903, he married Jessie Stewart. The couple had two daughters, Ruth and Esther. From 1907 to 1910 he served in the State Senate. In 1911 he became a U.S. District Attorney for the Eastern District of Michigan. On August 6, 1912 President William Howard Taft appointed him a U.S. District Judge for that same Eastern District of Michigan. Eighteen days later, on August 24, his wife, Jessie, died.

By political affiliation Judge Tuttle was a Republican, and over the years he assembled an impressive list of memberships in a variety of organizations. They included the Masons, Knight Templars, Shriners, Odd Fellows, Eagles, Elks, Macabbees, Woodmen, and Moose. He belonged to both the Detroit Golf Club and the Detroit Athletic Club.

His reputation for harsh sentences was well known. In 1930, in the closing days of prohibition he levied one of the largest liquor violation fines ever given. He had accepted the guilty please of two prominent restaurant owners and respected community leaders from Frankenmuth, Michigan; Herman Fischer and William Zehnder. They were both guilty of serving beer in their back dining rooms. Tuttle fined Fischer $10,000, Zehnder $5,000, and Zehnder's wife, Emily, 1 cent. The $10,000 fine was the maximum allowed by the law. This was for serving a few glasses of beer to some cronies in the back room at a time when the bootleggers in Detroit were transporting whisky across the border by the boatload and receiving lesser penalties. In 1930, the $10,000 and $5,000 fines brought both men close to financial ruin.[4]

Tuttle did agree to a reduction of $1,200 in both fines if Fischer and Zehnder would agree to having their beautiful carved oak bars smashed by Federal agents. They agreed and the Federal publicity stunt was staged, with photographers at the scene. At least one onlooker wept.[4]

Another of Judge Tuttle's well known cases was that of

Anthony Chebatoris who Tuttle had sentenced to hang for a murder committed in a Midland, Michigan bank robbery in 1937. Chebatoris had first fallen victim to a vigilant dentist, Dr. Frank Hardy, whose office was on the second floor of the building across the street from the Chemical State Bank of Midland, Michigan. Dr. Hardy had noticed that from his office he had an unusually fine view of the bank entrance and had commented to himself that if ever there was a holdup he would have a grandstand seat. Thinking about his ideal spot, he bought himself a rifle and kept it in the corner of the office where he worked on his patients' teeth. He had been duly deputized so that he could act in an official capacity.

Then one day Anthony Chebatoris and an accomplice entered the bank with the intention of robbing it. They killed a uniformed bank truck driver and wounded the bank president and a cashier. Dr. Hardy heard the shots and as the pair ran from the bank he shot and killed Chebatoris' accomplice and wounded Chebatoris. The fabled sheriff of Midland County, Ira M. Smith, who never carried a gun, cornered the wounded Chebatoris and persuaded him to surrender. Chebatoris was tried on a Federal charge, convicted, and sentenced to hang by Judge Tuttle. Since Chebatoris had murdered a bank guard, there was nothing excessively harsh in his penalty, it was what the law provided for and certainly Chebatoris deserved the maximum. When the sentence was carried out, Chebatoris set an unenviable record as being the first man to hang in Michigan where there was no State capital punishment. Despite the fact that the sentence was carried out under Federal law there was still some question about the legality of it taking place within the boundaries of Michigan at the Federal Penitentiary at Milan.

Much of the opposition to hanging Chebatoris in Michigan came from the 1937 Governor, Frank Murphy, who at the time of Stephan's case was a Supreme Court Justice mentioned in connection with William Nagel.

It all came down to one thing; Max Stephan could find little cause for optimism in the fact that his trial judge was to be Arthur J. Tuttle.

MAX STEPHAN'S FBI PHOTOGRAPH

On Monday, June 29, the trial opened with jury selection as the first order of business. Since it was a landmark case, willing jurors were not hard to find and at least a hundred people waited anxiously for the selection process. The key question asked of each was, "Do you feel that your verdict would be influenced by the knowledge that the maximum penalty for treason is death?" The question had to be answered, "No." In all, 14 jurors were rejected. Four were excused by the Court, eight were rejected by the defense and two by the Government. When the selection was complete, the jury was composed of six men and six women. It was said that several were of German descent and if names like Gerndt, Doensch, and Fischer are any clue, it must have been true.

The jury foreman was Jerry Armstrong, RFD 1, Emmett, Michigan. Emmett was, and still is, a small farming community about 17 miles west of Port Huron, on the main line of the Grand Trunk Western Railway. Armstrong wore an artificial hand that replaced a real one lost in a farm accident years before, during "hard times." He had given up farming and was a successful insurance man. Amberson, Stephan's attorney, had an arm problem also, although a temporary one. His arm was in a sling as a result of a fall from a porch a week earlier.

A court deputy issued fans to the six lady jurors, with a warning to leave them in the court room. Because of the hot weather the jurors were not to be locked up at night but instead were on their honor not to discuss the case with anyone. At the outset Judge Tuttle made it clear that the jury was not to concern itself with the fact that the crime in question carried a maximum penalty of death. The jury, he said, had no responsibility in the penalty. Their only job was to return a verdict of guilty or not guilty. He, and he alone, would bear the burden of responsibility for the penalty. The jury was under oath on that point.

The trial was rapidly turning into something like a county fair, complete with side shows, weirdos, kooks, and various hangers-on. People stood on railings and windowsills as they struggled to get a glimpse of someone or anyone. Through an apparent misunderstanding, Agnes Stephan was in the back of the courtroom on the first day. Later she learned that it was her right to sit with her husband, and on the second, third, and last day she sat at the defense table with Max. She, also, was receiving notoriety and refused to answer questions. Many people felt she had been told to stay silent because of her thick German accent. Both she and Max kept their faces covered with their hands, except in the courtroom. Agnes was dressed in an inexpensive silk dress with a blue silk coat. Prominently displayed on the coat was an American Red Cross pin. Her hair was gray and she wore a small black hat with white gardenias. The Detroit Times described her as a typical "hausfrau" and as stocky as Max himself. That was not quite fair. She was a nice looking lady, but maybe a few too many pork chops and potato pancakes had done their work on her figure and she was, indeed, overweight.

Finally, with the jury selected and everyone in their places it was time for the legal process to begin, one sided as it was.

Lehr made the opening remarks for the prosecution. He recounted the whole episode, telling how Krug found Mrs. Bertelmann and how Max Stephan became involved. He described the events of April 18th in detail, naming the people and places. Amberson declined to make an opening statement and the next order of business was the calling of the Government's witnesses.

Babcock, Lehr's assistant began. He was somewhat at a loss in regard to the correct legal procedure to use in putting his first point into the record. He began by saying he had a document to read. The document turned out to be a copy of the Declaration of War between Germany and the U.S. As he struggled with the legal procedure, Amberson came to his rescue. He said that he was willing to concede that Germany and the U.S. were at war. There was some bickering over the correct legal procedure for recognizing the state of war but it was finally settled and the Government proceeded to call its first witness.

He was George M. Read, Clerk of the Court for the judge who had sworn in the Stephans as citizens back in 1935. He had Stephan's naturalization papers with him and they became exhibits. Judge Tuttle explained how he hated to have his own official files marked with exhibit numbers and wanted to treat other judges files the same way. Therefore, no exhibit numbers were to be put on the documents. As if obsessed with the trivial, several minutes were spent deciding whether the unmarked exhibits were to be 1 and 2 or 1A and 1B. Tuttle preferred the former, saying that there were lots of numbers, but they became 1A and 1B. Finally, Read testified that Max Stephan had taken the oath of allegiance to the United States.

The Government called Peter Krug as its next witness. He was nattily attired in his standard *Luftwaffe* blue dress uniform. Under his jacket he wore the regulation white shirt and black tie. The silver cord around his jacket collar signified commissioned officer rank. On each lapel was an oak spray with two silver wings. His shoulders carried the single gold "pip" of an *Oberleutnant*; these were the ones that the Canadian jeweler had made. He carried his "Schirmmutze," the visored dress cap and his gloves under his arm and the FBI's gift dictionary in his hand as he entered the courtroom. The cap was piped in silver matching his collar. The focal point that people strained and hung from railings to see, however, was the insignia on his right breast. There, clutched by a *Luftwaffe* eagle, was the symbol of the Third Reich, the swastika, inside a small white circle. His cap carried the same symbol. A Detroit Times article described him as, "uniformed for a dress parade in the Fatherland." As he walked to the front of the courtroom he gave a Nazi salute to the bailiff who could only stare back in openmouthed astonishment. FBI agents rushed to intervene and the salute in the presence of the jury would long be discussed. Krug handed his hat and gloves to Bugas, almost, it was said, as though Bugas were his valet. Earlier when his name had been read, he smiled at the courtroom and gestured to himself, presumably to aid them in his identification. With him was Professor Joseph K.L. Bihl, professor of modern languages at the University of Detroit. He was to serve as interpreter in case Krug needed help either in understanding or expressing himself. Bihl had been born in Germany and had taught there.

The spectators were entranced as Krug took the stand and the questioning started. The first order of business with Krug, as with any other witness, was the swearing in. Krug balked somewhat at this. His first words were, "I can't swear under foreign law because I am a military man."

Tuttle replied, "Then you affirm. Our generous laws permit a witness to either take an oath or to affirm . . . "

Krug: I do not swear.
Tuttle: Use the word affirm.
Krug: Affirm, yes sir.

Babcock then began his questioning. Stephan smiled faintly when Krug looked at him and wondered what was about to happen. The initial questioning went;

Babcock: State your name.
Krug: *Oberleutnant* Hans Peter Krug

> Until then his first name was not public knowledge.
> Babcock: Now, you say "*Oberleutnant*," what is that, your official title.
> Krug: It is the official title of being an officer in the German Air Force.
> Babcock: That is of the Government of Germany?
> Krug: That is of the Government of Germany.

Under questioning Krug then related his capture in August, 1940 and his transfer to Camp W in Canada.

> Babcock: And that was an internment camp for war prisoners, was it?
> Krug: Yes, it seems to be.

After a few minutes Krug's nervousness disappeared and he began to take on an assured attitude. As the questioning proceeded he would sometimes refuse to answer on the grounds of military secrecy although those questions seemed to be almost irrelevant. He would freely answer the most damaging questions. Judge Tuttle was in a powerless position when Krug refused, since the Geneva Convention prevented him from taking any form of contempt action. Tuttle related how he had been in a similar position once before when two "lifers" from Jackson Prison were testifying. He could hardly increase their sentences. He even added that if anyone had a suggestion, he's be glad to listen to them.

Krug refused to tell how long he had been in the *Luftwaffe* but told of being a bomber pilot. He told of his transfer to Bowmanville, describing it as, "an officers' camp with some men to help us clean up around," referring to the company of enlisted men held there.

Babcock then questioned Krug about the escape. Krug, under questioning said, "I made my way out of camp." He refused to tell how he had escaped, saying that it was a military secret. Even though the dummy trick had been discovered, the workman trick had not. The Canadians still did not know how he had escaped. Several versions were written up at the time. One had him escaping in a packing crate, another as cutting through the wire. He described his encounter with the military policeman in the Toronto railway station and told how he was helped by the priest. The forged letters from the First Officer of the Normandie and the Postmaster of New York City were read and assigned exhibit numbers. The first of those documents showed his occupation to be that of "joiner." Judge Tuttle was fascinated by that. He told Babcock, "Be sure to ask him what a joiner is." Obediently, Babcock asked the question and Krug said that a joiner was a carpenter. Tuttle said he thought so, but it was an old-fashioned term that he had not heard recently.

Krug described the crossing of the Detroit River and his meeting with Mrs. Bertelmann. As he put it, he got her name from "comrades in camp." He told of Stephan being called and finally arriving. "Is Stephan here now?" asked Babcock.

Krug said, "Yes," and indicated Stephan with a nod of his head.

The questioning continued;

> Babcock: Did Mrs. Bertelmann have any money?
> Krug: Sure she had money. I guess she got some near the end of my visit. As I was leaving the house she took some money and gave it to me. It was $20 as far as I can remember. She gave me some socks, underwear, and a pair of shoes. I left the house with Stephan in his car.

That answer, of course, went far beyond Babcock's question and served to fully implicate Mrs. Bertelmann. Krug then described the drill at the restaurant when he went around the front to look like he was just arriving. He told of his walk in downtown Detroit and his trolley ride back. He smiled as he told of how he had asked the trolley conductor to stop at the U.S. Rubber Company. He described the scene when he returned, identifying all the things that Stephan had given him. The articles were duly marked as exhibits. A cornerstone question came next;

> Babcock: Now, do you mind stating what purpose you had in coming to the U.S., Lieutenant?

> Krug: My purpose was, one, to get through the U.S. and get back to Germany to do my duty again, and second to inform the German Government about all the things which happened during my time being a prisoner in the Canadian Camps. About bad conditions in Canada. About shooting and murdering one officer and four non-coms ranks and also about the things which happened when officers were caught in England and about the treatment of officers and men in Canadian camp.

The prosecution could do a lot with that statement. After all, he had said in front of everyone that he wanted to escape in order to rejoin the German armed forces. That answer served to assure the jury that, technically, they were indeed dealing with a case of treason. It was only the beginning for Krug. He would continue to make incriminating statements in connection with other participants.

Canadian authorities quickly refuted the charges of mistreatment and wanton shooting. There had been six cases of prisoners being killed by guards and each, they said, had been fully investigated by a court of inquiry and proven necessary to prevent escape. It is not known if the prosecution knew that Krug was going to condemn the Canadians, who were actually cooperating in bringing him to the trial. However, with the mistreatment issue now a matter of public record and widely reported in the U.S. it was virtually assured that by then, word had gotten back to Germany.

Reporters in democratic America commented on Krug's statement, too. When he mentioned the four noncoms they felt it was an afterthought. There were several theories in regard to why he was testifying and now people began to feel that he had a message to deliver and people like Stephan, were expendable.

Babcock questioned Krug about the clothes he was wearing during the escape. He said, "Where was your uniform, did you leave it in camp?"

Krug half rose at that. He was startled, but answered, "Yes." It looked like the espionage charge all over again. Technically, to be eligible for the protection of the Geneva Convention, it was required that one be in uniform. Some escapees did indeed wear their German uniform. By adding a different belt they could pose as a free Norwegian flyer. Generally, speaking, however, wearing a German uniform in an escape was out of the question and escapees simply wore civilian clothes and took their chances, or possibly as in Krug's case, carried an epaulet as a token uniform. The Germans were not as generous as the Canadians and Americans in their interpretation of this point. After one mass escape from Stalag Luft III they shot 50 British officers on this very point. The ashes of the 50 were returned to Stalag Luft III for burial and to serve as a warning.

Actually Krug may not have made out badly in his uniform. At the height of the war two actors in Detroit put on German uniforms and wandered around downtown. No one noticed them, or if they did, cared to do anything about it.

Under further questioning Krug told of the events of Saturday afternoon. He told of going with Stephan and waiting while he rented dishes. Babcock asked about Haller's;

> Babcock: What did you do at the restaurant?
> Krug: I sat down in a high chair, near, I don't know the word for it, near the counter and Stephan ordered two beers and two whiskies and each of us took one.

He told of forgetting the newly acquired bag, returning for it, and then going on to the Progressive Club. He described how he was introduced as a friend from Milwaukee.

The visit to Donay was also a key piece of testimony. He admitted telling Donay how many officers were in the Bowmanville camp, an allied military secret. He then told of the candy purchased for him and the conversation about von Werra. Asked if he knew who von Werra was, he said, "Yes, I knew him personally."

Krug then told of the visit to the "disorderly house" and the return to the restaurant. He told of registering at the hotel and of Stephan putting him on the bus the next morning.

At that point he was given an opportunity to describe the

story of his travels after Detroit. The story he told was a fairly elaborate cover story designed to protect the various people, particularly in Chicago, who had helped him. He said he was unsuccessful in making a contact in Chicago. While deciding what to do next, he said he read an article in a newspaper about a Swedish ship in New York that was to take German diplomatic personnel back to Germany, in exchange for our own. He thought, he said, that he might stow away on that ship. He claimed to have travelled to New York by bus, not untrue, but found that the ship would not sail for a long time. It was then, he said, that he decided to revert to his original plan of going to Mexico. From that point on, his courtroom itinerary was close to the real one. Dorothy and Margaret were ignored. The question of money cast suspicion on his story. Most people thought that he had little money when he arrived in Detroit. He could not have possibly travelled that far and bought the things he did, on the $40 that he received in Detroit. Therefore the question of money would continue to be pursued, but to no avail.

By then it was noon, Tuesday, the second day of the trial, and a recess was called until 2 P.M.

After the recess Krug answered a few more questions for Babcock. One dealt with whether or not he had ever heard of Stephan before the escape. He replied that he had not. Then it was Amberson's turn to cross examine.

Amberson was met with the "military secret" answer a few times in pursuing the question of how much money Krug had when he came to Detroit. A few questions later he asked Krug how much money he had when he left Detroit. Krug said, "If I told you that you would know how much I had when I came." The FBI agents got a chuckle out of that one.

The questions continued;

> Amberson: Will you define to this jury what you mean by "military secret" as an officer of the German *Luftwaffe*?

A translation was requested.

Krug: A military secret: when we make an escape all the facts in connection with an escape are military secrets because every single thing which we do and which happens during an escape gives information to the enemy, how we handle such an escape and how we are able to escape and how we are able to make our way to the States and so on.

Amberson asked about the visit to the "disorderly house" which he called a "bawdy house." This also required help from the interpreter. Krug replied, "I can't see any connection with the question."

Amberson: Well, you did visit such a place, didn't you?
Krug: Oh, I did.
Amberson: And had intercourse with a prostitute?
Krug: Wait a minute, I beg your honor that I am not questioned in this manner.

Krug was flushed and embarrassed. Tuttle said that he couldn't see anything wrong with the question since the same one had been asked previously by the prosecution. Krug said, "Yes, but in a far better manner." Tuttle went on to explain that manners or not, Amberson was defending his host of some two months earlier and it would behoove him to cooperate.

On several occasions in the trial, Tuttle had become angered at Krug's comments. One time his face turned red and he turned to Krug saying, "Young man, in U.S. courts the judge is in the habit of deciding legal questions."

Krug finished testifying on the various points of who paid who for what and when. The questioning continued:

Amberson: Did you steal that rowboat?
Krug: I didn't steal it but I took it.

The FBI agents and other spectators in the courtroom laughed out loud at this answer and Tuttle became angered. He threatened to clear the courtroom if they did not behave themselves. In answering this question Krug had alluded to a point in international law dealing with prisoners. Prisoners could not be charged with theft in taking articles to be used in escapes. The provision had its reasons. It was to prevent a prisoner from being returned to an enemy country on a minor theft charge. It had been a factor in the von Werra case which happened while the U.S. was neutral. Von Werra also "took" a rowboat.

Amberson asked if he had any help in crossing the Detroit River. Krug said he had come across the river by himself.

> Amberson: And underneath your coveralls did you have a suit of clothes and a pair of pants?
> Krug: I can't tell you, its a military secret.
> Amberson: A military secret, well now suppose we touch on the subject of underwear, would that be a military secret? Did you have on underwear?
> Krug: Of course I had underwear.
> Amberson: That is somewhere between a pair of pants and underwear is a line of demarcation between military secrets and what can be told, is that true?
> Krug: Yes, because . . .
> Amberson: All right.
> Krug: Nobody goes through the streets in underwear.
> Amberson: In underwear, however, you got a suit of underwear at Mrs. Bertelmann's, didn't you?
> Krug: Yes, I did.

Under questioning Krug then told of buying the pistol and ammunition.

> How much money did you have when you arrived in San Antonio?
> Krug: That is a military secret.
> Amberson: Why did you buy the pistol?
> Krug: Because it looked nice and it was cheap and I would like to have it for a souvenir.
> Amberson: (Holding up cartridges) Well these were souvenirs also?
> Krug: Yes, to make some practice when I went back to Germany again.

Amberson: For target practice?
Krug: It was my idea.

Amberson then asked Krug if he had carried a Luger pistol when he was a pilot. Krug said that he did not, he carried a Mauser. Amberson asked him his military unit and Krug refused to answer. Amberson then said, "Your rank is now that of *Oberleutnant*?" Krug replied in the affirmative. Amberson asked, "Do I pronounce it correctly?" He then repeated it several times and Krug testified that it was a correct pronunciation. Krug told of his promotion and how there was no connection between it and his escape.

Krug described his escape preparation, claiming to have made up the name of Jean Etté and to have typed the false credentials on camp typewriters. He described his education and his entry into the *Luftwaffe*. He told of how the Canadian Government paid him $21.40 a month while a prisoner. Tuttle was intrigued by this. He said to Amberson, "Ask him if Canada had to pay him more because of his promotion."

He told how Donay had given him $20 out of his "casket" and how Stephan had given him money to pay the prostitute. Upon recapture, Krug tried to chew up little pieces of cardboard with names and addresses on them. They had been taken from him, partly chewed, and were exhibits at the trial. Amberson questioned him about them;

Amberson: In regard to the piece of cardboard . . .
Krug: I can't tell you what it says.
Amberson: It's in German, German script.
Krug: Yes.
Amberson: You can't read it?
Krug: No, I won't read it.
Amberson: Did Max Stephan say that he wanted you to enjoy your stay in Detroit and make it pleasant for you?
Krug: Yes, that is right.
Amberson: Did you know that Stephan was a citizen?
Krug: No, I didn't ask him.
Amberson: Weren't you interested?
Krug: I wasn't informed about citizenship and so on.

The FBI agents in San Antonio had told Krug about Stephan and the fact that he was a citizen and in deep trouble.

Amberson: Do you know Mr. Bugas of the FBI?
Krug: Yes, I know him.
Amberson: Did you make a statement to him in writing and sign you name to it?
Krug: No.
Amberson: Did you make a statement to Mr. Lehr or Babcock?
Krug: Yes, wait a minute, that was here in this building. (At the indictment)
Amberson: Did the defendant, Max Stephan, at any time say to you that he wanted to destroy the Government of the United States?
Krug: He wants to destroy the Government?
Amberson repeated the question.
Krug: No, he never said that to me.
Amberson: Did you study Latin?
Krug: Language?
Amberson: Latin.
Krug: No.

Amberson then went into a lengthy discussion with the interpreter about the word "subvert" and its German equivalent. The interpreter said that while there was no direct equivalent, certainly the meaning could be expressed in German. There was then a discussion between the interpreter and Krug. At its conclusion the interpreter told Amberson that Krug knew exactly what "subvert" meant.

Amberson: Did Max Stephan say that he wanted to bring about a subversion of the American Government?
Krug: No, he didn't tell me anything about it.
Amberson was hardly getting good answers from Krug, partly because of Krug's limited knowledge of English.
Amberson: Did you say anything to him about destroying the American form of government.
Krug: No.

Amberson: Have you been made any promise of parole by the British Government because of your testimony?
Krug: No, they didn't do anything.
Amberson: Do you expect any special treatment from the Canadian Government?
Krug: No.
Amberson: Now, did you request of Max Stephan at any time during the conversation, any aid from him for the Government of Germany except as it applied to you individually?

The point of the question was clear to most, but Krug needed help from the interpreter.

Krug: No, I didn't.
Amberson: And that was not your purpose in talking to Max Stephan, was it?
Krug: No.
Amberson: To secure aid for the Government of Germany?
Krug: It was just my purpose to get back to Germany again.
Amberson: And it was not your purpose to tear down the Government of the United States, was it?
Krug: Of course not.

Amberson had, of course, made few points for his client with that line of questioning. Everyone knew why Krug wanted to get back; Krug had stated it several times in answers to different questions. Amberson took a new tack;

Amberson: Now, you stand today in this courtroom, witness, as an enemy of our country, that is true, is it?
Krug: Yes, it is.
Amberson: And those of us here in this courtroom, we are your enemies, that is true, is it not?
Krug: Of course you are.
Amberson: You understand from your knowledge of international law that no power on earth can make you testify in this lawsuit unless you wanted to, you know that?
Krug: That is right.

Amberson: Will you state to the jury, then, what is your purpose in coming here as an enemy of this country and testifying in this case against a man who is charged with treason against our country, what is your purpose, your object?
Krug: The purpose is to clear out that he didn't do what he is charged with. I was only asked to tell the truth about the case and what is wrong. What FBI has charged him and all the other persons who are charged with knowing who I am.

Amberson was obviously trying to get a message through to Krug.

Amberson: In other words, witness, if I understand you correctly, you feel now as a witness here that the defendant, Max Stephan did not do the things he is charged with here in doing, is that correct?

Both Lehr and Babcock objected simultaneously at that question. Judge Tuttle sustained their objection and explained to Amberson, "You can't ask him, in a sense—what do you think, is he guilty or not." It made no difference to Amberson. He was done with Krug. However, Babcock wanted to re-question Krug on one or two points. He began his redirect examination.

Babcock clarified a few minor points in regard to the Luger and Mauser pistols and the gifts that Stephan had given him. He then questioned Krug about the discussion in Donay's store, particularly about the officer being shot. Krug then turned to Judge Tuttle;

Krug: Your honor, would you be good enough to answer a question. You see I don't know what he is called. [Krug was trying to refer to Amberson but did not know his title.]
Judge Tuttle: How is that, I don't understand you?
Krug: The defender of Max Stephan told me that if I stayed and testified against Stephan. If that is so I will be relieved from further questioning because it is not the

intention—it is not my—I don't intend to testify against Stephan. I was told by the FBI agents that I have only to clear out the facts and to tell the truth and nothing but the truth.
Judge Tuttle: That is what you are sworn to do and that is as far as I have to do with it. I have nothing to do with whom the testimony helps or who it harms. My only desire is that people tell the truth. This is what you took your affirmation to do, not oath but affirmation, to tell the truth and so that is what I say to you, you should do is tell the truth. You may go ahead.
Krug: Yes, I have another objection. I asked the FBI agents that I never can testify against a man who helped me but they told me about when I made this question that there is no testimony against him but only in statement of the facts he has already told.

Babcock had no further questions for Krug anyway, at that point. This was followed by a discussion of what to do with Krug. Amberson said that he may want to question him again. Actually, Amberson simply overlooked his golden opportunity at this point. Krug had begun to balk. Had Amberson followed up with more questioning and Krug had refused to answer, Krug's entire testimony would have to be thrown out and possibly a mistrial could have been declared. Amberson did not pursue that line of reasoning, however.

Tuttle was concerned about the hardships they were working on the Canadian authorities and asked a Canadian officer if they could bring Krug back again on request, if necessary. The Canadian officer told the Judge, "I will, sir." Judge Tuttle told Krug that he was dismissed.

Krug: Thanks, your honor.
Judge Tuttle: What is the book you have, young man?
Interpreter: That is a dictionary.
Judge Tuttle: Dictionary? What dictionary have you got?
Krug: English -German, German -English.
Judge Tuttle: Who wrote it, who wrote it?
Interpreter: It seems to be Cassells.

> Judge Tuttle: All right, I was just curious to know what the book was that he was carrying around.
> Interpreter: It is Broyer.

The FBI agents may have had a few anxious moments over that exchange. It may not have looked too good for them if Krug's friendly inscription on the front page were read into the trial record.

Krug's testimony on the witness stand lasted a total of four hours, starting on Monday and ending on Tuesday. In that short period of time the *Oberleutnant* had become a focal point of interest.

One of his Canadian guards even received a bit of publicity that he probably would have preferred to avoid. On Monday night, following the first part of Krug's testimony, Private Joseph Mullen was presumably minding his own business at the corner of Columbia and Hastings in downtown Detroit. He was accosted by a "Negro" woman and mugged by several men. In his words, he was "strong-armed." Some people gave him first aid in a drug store on Gratiot and he was taken to Receiving Hospital. His injuries included lacerations of the forehead and other bruises. He reported to police that he had been robbed of $17.50(US), his furlough card, and his false teeth. It is doubtful that he received any Canadian equivalent to the Purple Heart in that action.

Krug was still the focal point and people wanted to know more about him. Jane Schermerhorn, a feature writer for the Detroit Times caught much of the feeling in her July 2nd article. That was a Thursday and actually the last day of the trial but she was discussing events of two days earlier. In typical newspaper fashion at the time, she put it into words;

"Max is the forgotten man. He is playing a supporting role to the swashbuckling *Luftwaffe Oberleutnant* Hans Peter Krug. Stephan should be the center of attraction, his life hangs in the balance, but everyone watches the blue-uniformed, heel clicking Krug, his imperious Nazi Officer bearing that quiets the courtroom when he enters and leaves." Schermerhorn went on to discuss Krug, "For Krug is Detroit's first contact with the enemy and the crowd studies his every movement like an army of biologists confronted by a new species of animal."

The interest in Krug inspired Schermerhorn to interview Krug's interpreter, Professor Bihl, in order to find out more about this new species of bug. The professor was obviously saddened by what he could see had happened to youth in his native country. Schermerhorn asked Bihl if Krug was an exceptional person. He said, "No, he is very average. He had what compares to our high school education, but he is Nazi youth. Glibly he can cite international law and he is cognizant of his rights as a military officer. That is what German youth is taught today. No longer in Germany do children sing folk songs, revel in fairy tales. No, Krug as a representative of German youth saddens me. No, he is very average, very German."

Actually the good professor was wrong on one point. The German military was not really schooled in international law and prisoner rights. Such education was considered bad for morale. Krug learned about that in camp.

The professor's real error, however, was in calling Krug average. The escape and his travels were certainly not the work of an average man. It had taken wits, resourcefulness, guts, and of course, the kind of luck that comes from hard work. Krug claims to have felt that it would be best if he conducted himself in an "average way." The ironic part was that the Professor scared more people by saying that Krug was average, than if he had said he was exceptional. My God, people thought, if he is one of the average ones, how long will this war last? Were they really, as Hitler claimed, a super race after all? The thought passed through people's minds.

While being held out of court in FBI headquarters, Krug managed to make more news. Apparently one of the FBI agents invited a friend, Detroit advertising executive Frank J. Mullen, in to meet the celebrity. Krug was quoted as having contempt for the U.S. press and newspapermen in general. He said, "I do not like newspapermen, they write too much."

Frank Mullen replied sarcastically, "Some people talk too much." It was starting to come out, that old American trait that no matter what, you just don't "squeal" on your friends. Maybe the American attitude came from a steady diet of 1930 era movies, the ones about gangsters. Usually there was a prison scene, maybe with James Cagney. The "squealer" or "stool pigeon" was some little weasel faced snitch who met his demise by being processed through the industrial size clothes wringer in the prison laundry or maybe was crushed by a slab of boiler plate in the prison workshop. By now, Detroiters would have gladly watched both Krug and Stephan disappear through the rollers of that prison clothes wringer.

Maybe it also had to do with sympathy for the underdog. Stephan didn't stand a chance and Krug was jumping on him when he was down. People felt that Krug was stabbing Stephan in the back. As the victim, Stephan was almost becoming a pitiable character, to have been betrayed so completely by someone he had helped.

But it was too late for pity and the trial continued, even though, as the saying goes, Krug was a tough act to follow. The next witness called by the prosecution was Canadian Captain William Henry Atkey. He was the camp dental officer who had taken the roll when the dummies were detected. In reply to Babcock's questions he attested to the escape and was asked if the Krug he knew was the same person who had been on the stand earlier. Atkey replied, "Yes, quite definitely."

Amberson cross examined. Atkey declined to tell how many prisoners were confined at Bowmanville on the basis that it was a military secret. Krug had previously testified that the number was about 500, not that it seemed to matter. Atkey told of Krug's dental appointments and explained how a civilian interpreter had helped with the identification.

Next was Staff Sergeant Cecil John Rule who had been with Atkey during the roll call. He explained his duties as senior NCO in the enclosure. His job, he said was to maintain discipline and count prisoners. Undoubtedly the prisoners had some uncomplimentary nickname for him, as they had for most in his position. ("Fruitnose" was the one at Gravenhurst Barracks.)[10] He told how the prisoners stood in rows, five yards apart while he counted them. He described the dummies with their red faces and their stiff black hair. He told of re-counting and finding the camp two prisoners short. Amberson cross examined Rule. He asked if he had talked to Krug when he was returned after recapture. Rule said that they weren't allowed to talk to the prisoners except in the direct line of duty, a regulation aimed at preventing friendships from forming. Rule did report that Krug said to him, "Hello, sergeant, I have had a nice trip."

Rule said to him, "Where have you been?"

Krug replied, "I cannot tell."

The prosecution then called Joseph W. McGuire. He had seen Stephan and Krug together at the Progressive Club and testified accordingly. In cross examination Amberson asked if the Progressive Club was private or public. He was told that it was "semi-public, but anyone could go there." McGuire said under questioning that there had been no conversation between himself and Stephan or Krug. He was probably grateful to Amberson for the opportunity to distance himself from the whole affair.

Next on the prosecution's list was William Lenz. He told of renting dishes to Max Stephan and of calling the railway station regarding trains to Chicago. He testified to telling Max Stephan the times and the fare. Amberson had no questions in cross examination.

Babcock then called August Haller, the tavern operator. He told of Max Stephan entering his establishment between 3 and 4 o'clock on April 18th. He attested to Krug having been described as "one of Meier's boys."

Judge Tuttle contributed a few distractions at that point. The windows were open due to the hot weather and the street traffic made hearing difficult. Also, he had to excuse himself for a few minutes. It was, he explained, the end of the fiscal year for the court and he had to see an attorney for a minute. He returned and the questioning continued.

Under Babcock's questioning, Haller told of how Krug forgot his bag and returned for it. Then it was Amberson's turn. He found that Haller had known Stephan for 10 years, that there had been no attempt to conceal Krug, and a few trivial facts—he had been in business five and one half years.

Next was Walter Emerick, the clerk at the Field Hotel. He identified Krug as one of his April 18th guests. Asked if he saw Max Stephan, he replied, "I seen him after this boy registered in, about 11." Asked, "What did you say?" he gave his remark made to Stephan, "I've got half a hunch that I just checked in a German flier."

He told Max's answer, "Maybe so, you can't tell." Amberson cross-examined. He asked Emerick if he told Stephan about the two dots over the "u" that Krug had used when he registered as "Müller." He said he had not mentioned that.

Judge Tuttle broke in at that point. He wanted to know if at that time Emerick knew the connection between Stephan and Krug. He asked if it was just a coincidence that he stopped by. Emerick replied, "Yes." Babcock came back in redirect examination. He verified that Emerick did not know that Stephan had sent Krug to the hotel.

The next two witnesses were Karl and Eva Erhardt. Karl had been called back from Jefferson Barracks in Missouri where he was training as an airman. He testified to the Saturday night visit to the restaurant in which he paid the bill for the wedding party. Both he and Eva told of being sent over to see the "friend from Milwaukee" and of sitting with him while he was eating and drinking.

It was then Tuesday afternoon and court was adjourned until 9:30 A.M. the next day, July 1.

When court reopened, Eva Erhardt was called back to verify Krug's identity. Krug was brought in and she said, "Yes, that is the man."

The next witness was Erna Schwartz, the waitress. She said she saw Krug sitting in the front part of the restaurant and asked Stephan who he was. She said she was told, "A German fellow from Canada." She testified that Stephan asked her where she thought he should put Krug up for the night. She claimed to have made an offer, saying she had an empty room in "mine house" where he could stay for one night. She further testified that Stephan said, "I think he can go to the Field Hotel to sleep." She asked Krug if he was ready to leave and when he replied that he was, she showed him how to get to the hotel. Further, she testified to having seen Mrs. Bertelmann the next day and claimed to have said nothing.

Amberson cross-examined at length. He asked her about her family and her background. She claimed to have learned Krug's name in the papers. She told of having served the food to Krug, also telling the court what she had served. There were, she said, about 15 people in the restaurant when Krug was there. She told of the Bund meetings, none of which had been held since the war, she said. Babcock came back in re-direct examination in which he asked about the Bund association.

The prosecution then called another of its key witnesses, Mrs. Margareta Johanna Bertelmann. She had been brought to the trial from her new home, the detention camp for enemy aliens. That was to be her home until the end of the war when she would face deportation. She cried throughout a great deal of her testimony. She told the story of how Krug came to her flat and how she called Max Stephan. She told of her emotions at the time and of Stephan's reaction to her emotions. She told of overhearing Krug tell of his Detroit River crossing. She heard Stephan suggest to Krug that he give himself up and she told of hearing Krug's answer. She told of Stephan's call to her on Sunday when he insisted that she work as a waitress that evening in his restaurant. She was extremely nervous and when asked how far it was from her flat to Stephan's she asked, "By car or streetcar?" She told of the packages to the prisoners, including the part about buying tobacco wholesale from Stephan.

Amberson gleaned more information from her about her past. She told of Krug not feeling well and of the plate of food that she had placed in front of him. Then she told of being taken to FBI headquarters on the night of April 19th, explaining that she was not arrested at that time. She testified that the Sunday meeting was that of the Steuben Society. She was confused on that point. It was the Schwaben Society. She went on to refer to the Steuben Society as the Steuben Verein and said that it was an old, old German society. The meeting on the 19th of April was actually their spring festival, she said.

Before she was dismissed, Judge Tuttle had a few points on his mind, also. He asked her whose money it was that she had given to Krug. She said it was her own. It was, she said, part of the money that her daughter regularly gave to her for room and board. Tuttle probed further. He asked why she had been afraid when Krug came to her flat. Was it, he asked, because she was afraid that Krug might harm her in some way. No, she told the Judge, it was because the police might find him there.

The prosecution then called the two lady entertainers, starting with Alvina Ludlow. She pointed out Max Stephan and told of Krug being with him. She implicated "Peggy" Merrifield. Amberson did not let her off as lightly as Babcock. He asked her about her "house," how many rooms, how many vacancies, any arrests, and other probing questions. She said she could not remember ever having been arrested but said she had been put on probation once. Judge Tuttle intervened to explain the mystery she had posed in that reply.

Amberson asked if Merrifield was white or colored. "White," she said. She explained that Krug and Merrifield were only in the bedroom a minute or so and that she was told by Merrifield that the party didn't like her and wouldn't even talk to her.

Next, Ethel "Peggy" Merrifield was called. Again Babcock was brief. She gave her address and identified Krug and Stephan. Amberson again probed more deeply. After a few "backgrounders" about her marital status and other vital statistics he asked about the call from Mrs. Ludlow:

> Amberson: Do you know what she wanted you to do at her house?
> Merrifield: Well, I had an idea.
> Amberson: Well, what was that idea?
> Merrifield: Well, I was to entertain one of these boys.
> Amberson: And what do you mean by entertain?
> Merrifield: Well, must I go into that?
> Judge Tuttle: Yes.

Merrifield: Intercourse with him.
Amberson: You mean sexual intercourse?
Merrifield: Yes sir, with one of the men.

She then testified that she had been with Krug about five minutes and had gotten three dollars.

The next witness was Dietrich Rintelin, Donay's clerk. His testimony was short. He simply testified to seeing Stephan and Krug together in the store. He told of snatches of conversation he had heard and of the expressions on everyone's faces. Amberson had no questions. It was never brought out that he was an FBI informant and the one who had called the FBI that Saturday.

The prosecution was getting near the end of its list of witnesses. Remaining were three FBI agents. The first was Lawrence Gasteiger, actually a lab technician. He had examined all the papers, chewed and otherwise, found on Krug. Under his direction the FBI lab technicians had reconstructed most of the paper that Krug had chewed. This much could be made out, said Gasteiger;

"Hotel Manchan
George E. Mann
Antigua Guatemala C.A.

Hotel __za
W__da Yucatan
__co City"

Amberson had no questions for him.

Next called was Jack O. Parker, the San Antonio FBI agent who had gone to the Nueces Hotel and arrested Krug. The arrest had been at 11:55 P.M. he said, and he told the names of the others who had been with him. He told of knocking on the door and later, of examining Krug's papers. He told of the police officer finding the gun in the room and of finding a map marked with Krug's route. Parker testified to being told by Krug that he had accomplished one of his escape objectives.

Amberson then cross-examined. He got closer to finding out how much money Krug had with him when he came to

Detroit. It will be recalled that earlier, in examining Krug, Amberson had failed on that point; Krug had refused to answer. Parker testified that Krug had $33 when he was captured. Krug's finances continued to be an important point. It was well established that he had received $40 and some odd cents in Detroit and had spent a few dollars. He had travelled from Detroit to Chicago, then to New York, and then to San Antonio. He had spent about $15 on a gun and ammunition. Most people felt that he had little money with him when he left camp, which led to the further conclusion that his expenditures did not check out with his income. Nevertheless, the question was not pursued further. What no one knew was that when they had searched Krug in San Antonio they had missed $125 that he had hidden away and which he carried back to camp.

Babcock then called John Bugas who told of arresting Stephan. He testified to advising him of his rights and to taking the statement from him. It was the prosecution's intention to place the statement in evidence as an exhibit but Amberson objected. The jury was directed to leave the courtroom while a discussion was held on the admissibility of it. Tuttle overruled the objection with Amberson taking exception for the record. Tuttle then, in his words, sent for the "fourteen good and true," twelve jurors plus two alternates. The statement was given an exhibit number and Bugas read it into the record. As mentioned earlier, there was little about the episode that it did not say.

Amberson cross-examined Bugas and found out about his trips to Canada to talk with Krug in order to sell him on the idea of testifying.

The Government announced, at that point, that it had no more witnesses to call.

Surprisingly, Amberson announced that the defense would call no witnesses. Not even Max Stephan would take the stand in his own defense. Amberson was, of course, not about to let Stephan be cross-examined by Babcock.

Amberson then made a motion for a directed verdict of "not guilty." The basis of the plea was that the Government had failed to prove;

1. That Stephan was guilty by evidence,
2. that Stephan was a U.S. citizen, and
3. that he had acted with wrongful intent.

The citizenship question was based on a defense contention that the picture on Stephan's naturalization papers did not look like him. It was nothing more than a formality. In denying all three pleas, Judge Tuttle said that the picture looked like Stephan to him. The jury was out of the room during that exchange.

By then it was Wednesday afternoon and the court was adjourned until the next day. Agnes' eyes were red from the strain. The couple ate lozenges in rapid succession. Max had not been allowed to see any papers and he was concerned with how they were treating him.

When court reconvened on Thursday, apparently Judge Tuttle had been doing some thinking overnight. He sent the jury out while he held a discussion with the lawyers. Tuttle was concerned with several points. Foremost was the testimony of Ludlow and Merrifield. For some reason he wanted their testimony stricken from the case as well as the overt act that referred to the visit to the house of prostitution. In terms of relevance, that visit certainly ranked with Haller's and the Progressive Club, but Tuttle didn't like it. He said it couldn't possibly be of any aid and comfort to Germany. The implication was that in this supposedly important case he did not want any testimony of that type if he could possibly avoid it. He may have thought of this as being some kind of landmark case that would be read and studied, maybe even by impressionable young children, and it needed to be sanitized. Tuttle referred to Ludlow and Merrifield as, "those two ladies, if we can call those two creatures ladies." The prosecution reluctantly went along with Tuttle.

Part of the testimony of Jack Parker, the San Antonio FBI agent was also stricken on a technicality. It was the part dealing with what Krug had said to him after being arrested.

The jury was called back in and told to disregard the

stricken testimony. Both sides were then ready for oral arguments.

Babcock summarized the Government's case. His remarks became so devastating at times that the Stephans lost their composure. It was July 2nd when he made his summarization and, with the 4th only two days away, he did not miss the chance to make reference to it, " . . . take a little trip in fantasy to the city of Philadelphia and there let us walk up the steps of Independence Hall."

There was an interruption at that point. They noticed that Amberson had not yet returned from recess. He came through the door and Tuttle explained what had happened, offering to have Babcock's remarks read back. Amberson, perhaps realizing that whatever he had said, it would do no good to have the jury hear it twice, said, "No, I know anything he said was alright."

Babcock continued, describing the scene at the signing of the Declaration of Independence. "What makes that room so hallowed," he asked, "a walk to the showcase tells us why."

" . . . and now come with me again to another solemn moment in another sacred place. A court room of a U.S. District Court; 159 years after this Declaration of Independence was signed and announced to the world, this defendant, Max Stephan, on June 24, 1935 stood in a room among a group of people petitioning the gracious government of the U.S. to be admitted to the honor of U.S. citizenship. There was a hush of silence . . . Max Stephan raised his right hand." Babcock told of the seven years that Stephan had been a citizen and, "breathed the free air of American liberty." He said that all Stephan had to do on that day in April was to make a phone call. He spoke of Stephan's love for the "Vaterland" and said, "For only a traitorous heart can commit treason." He repeated a remark made by Stephan to Mrs. Bertelmann, "are you crazy," explaining that only in Stephan's traitorous frame of mind would her reaction be considered crazy. "His was a treason controlled heart," said Babcock. "You can't get away with it," Babcock erroneously claimed was what Stephan said to Krug.

That remark, said Babcock, should have been said by Stephan to himself.

Babcock then reviewed the events of the 18th of April. One by one he ticked off the visits the pair had made. He picked up one of the exhibits, the Greyhound map, and passed it among the jury. "Note," he said, "the line on the map is continuous, not drawn as he went, drawn ahead of time." That was not true, of course. The line was simply drawn after Krug found the map.

"Guilty as charged, you should say to Max Stephan, down through the years ahead which your normal flaccid physique will probably give you in the future, down through the years ahead which your apparently phlegmatic nervous system prognosticates, remember, remember, you can't get away with it." There was one subtle point here. The jury was being told that Stephan would spend the rest of his life in jail for his crime.

It was just before noon on Thursday when Babcock concluded his summary and Tuttle asked Amberson if he would prefer to start after lunch. Amberson took that option and court was recessed and then reconvened at 1 o'clock.

In the sarcasm department Amberson was easily the equal of Babcock. He began, "May it please your honor, members of the jury. I liked the opening argument of Mr. Babcock. It was a fine effort. I liked especially the reference he made to the signing of the Declaration of Independence. Was Babcock thinking of the country which spawned his star witness, Krug—ours a government of the law, Krug's a government of one man, government of a beast . . . "

"He is not the first German Officer I have seen, in another war I talked to German officers. I never thought I would live to see the day when a representative of our country says, thank you, Lieutenant, will you please do that, Lieutenant. That wasn't the language we used to use . . . "

Amberson explained why Stephan had not been brought to the stand, "there is no dispute, every act proven is admitted." He then discussed the events of the Saturday, the drinks, the food, and the bus. "There is only one question," said Amberson, "did he intend to subvert the Government of the United

States? I will concede that it was foolish and silly. I will concede that what he did was unmoral, if you know what I mean."

Amberson then took issue with a key point of Babcock's argument. He said, "I must, I do this and I do it regretfully. I must accuse my brother Babcock of deliberately misquoting the testimony. 'You can't get away with it,' which he attributed to Stephan was in fact not supported by the record." Amberson went on, "Now what did Mr. Stephan say to Mr. Bugas, the bright young man who heads the FBI here?" He then read from the statement to which Stephan had claimed to have said, "I told him it was impossible to do and to go back where he came from."

Amberson mentioned the Nazi salute that Krug had given upon entering the courtroom. He reminded the jury that Krug had refused to take an oath. As Amberson put it, "God Almighty has been abolished in Germany." He told the story of the Good Samaritan, saying, "I read that over last night and I thought to myself, just as sure as God made little apples, if the FBI had been operating in Palestine between Jerusalem and Jericho on that occasion they would have had that Samaritan in the highest court in Jerusalem and charged with treason because he befriended an enemy traveller." He made the point that Krug was not acting on orders of superior officers and that made a difference.

There had already been several implications that certain government people were using the case to build their own reputations. In his closing statement Amberson alluded to that as well as to his own reasons for taking the case:

"They say great oaks from little acorns grow, and sometimes, you know, in the pursuance of ambitions, mountains are made out of mole hills. But this is a court of justice. This is not a place for the creation of something to point back at in the future and say, 'I accomplished that.' This is a place where Judge Tuttle and John Lehr and John Babcock and I and Johnny Bugas, the chief of the FBI and you and I, we are all working together here to solve this problem of responsibility. It is not a one man responsibility. It is not the responsibility of the court alone, nor that of the District Attorney. And what does that responsibility entail on us? That we be fair, and that we be decent . . . "

Certainly reputations were made in such cases. One could go down in history in this one and conviction was almost assured. Stephan, through his own stupidity, had virtually handed it to them.

Amberson continued, "I suppose I could do in this case, as I have done before and as other lawyers have done, I could make an appeal to your sympathy. And I want to say to you, speaking for this respondent, we don't want any sympathy in this lawsuit." Amberson probably realized that Stephan, with his unsavory reputation, really didn't evoke much sympathy in anyone, anyway. He went on, "I believe as a lawyer that I am right in this case, and if I didn't believe I was right, I would have put the respondent upon the witness stand."

"I believe I am right as to the law. I have no fears whatever as to what the law is that is going to be given you by Judge Tuttle, because I know what it is. No fear of that. And I have no fear that there is any possibility that this proof all put together shows a wicked, evil, and malicious intent to destroy this government . . . "

"I will concede that the actions of this man were foolish. I will say that they were silly, they were wrong, they were unmoral . . . "

"Let us not, in this time of stress, in this time of war, make our determinations in a court of justice from our emotions. As Winston Churchill said a few months ago in addressing the House of Commons, 'Keep your eyes on the stars, your head in the clouds, and your feet on the ground.' He said that is the way to win this war, and I say that is the way to decide a lawsuit of this character . . . "

"My responsibility has about ceased. I have done the best I could. Some of my friends in and out of the profession, when it was disclosed that I was of record as the attorney for Max Stephan, were kind or unkind enough to criticize me for defending a man charged with treason. Why, I said, it is the very foundation of our government . . . "

"And I have no apologies to make for Max Stephan, and no apologies to make for appearing in this case. And I have no apologies to make to Berlin for insulting Lieutenant Krug. Thank you."

Amberson's defense was closed at that point and about all we can conclude is that it was less than brilliant. He had failed to follow-up on Krug's balky behavior, had apparently done little research, and had not called any witnesses. On this last point, there were perfectly normal people who liked Stephan. It may have been difficult to get any of them as character witnesses but he should have had someone who could, at least, say something good about his client. Maybe none of that would have helped, but it just seems that more effort should have been put forth.

All that was left at that point was the closing argument on behalf of the government. Lehr, himself, was to handle that job. He started out with a reference to the "soul stirring speech of my learned brother." Getting to the point, he said, "There is no degree of treason, no degree, because the gist is a breach of allegiance." He reminded the jury that when Stephan took his oath to become a citizen he renounced allegiance to any foreign power, particularly Germany.

"I can see cases where great harm was done and the death penalty would be proper and then I can see other cases of treason where the damage was not much because it was stopped in time before it was carried out, where the death penalty would be absolutely unfair," Lehr said, in an apparent softening. That last remark seems strange in the midst of phrases about blackhearted traitors. In one respect it sounded like an appeal to any of the jurors who might have been reluctant to return a guilty verdict because of the possibility of a death penalty, which they might have felt was too severe. Judge Tuttle had hardly given any signs of leniency. In reality, Lehr was expressing his own opinion, held secretly until then, that Stephan, while guilty of treason, did not deserve to die for his crime.

Lehr was also anxious to get back at Amberson for implying that the prosecution had, in essence, kowtowed to Krug. "Who is Krug," he said, "he is Max Stephan's friend." He went on, "Why didn't he bring some witnesses to contradict what Krug said?" Amberson objected to that.

Lehr went on, "Was Krug playing hookey, was poor dumb Max, good generous Max, only helping this boy home to his mother and father? Remember who Krug was. Krug was piloting a bomber for the purpose of killing innocent men and women. I presume if he could make his way he would come over here and be bombing the United States of America. What would you have done, would you have fed, clothed? Max's duty was to call the police, but he failed to do it." Lehr went into the contrast between Mrs. Bertelmann and Stephan. She, Lehr said, was scared, Stephan was happy.

Lehr also felt it was necessary to draw a distinction between helping an enemy in a treasonable as opposed to non-treasonable way. The defense had raised that point originally. Lehr said, "A Jap might fly over here across the Pacific in a bomber and crash and be injured. It is not treason to drag him from the plane but that is not what Max Stephan did."

Lehr brought his own background into the summation, telling the jury that his own father had come to this country from Germany. He closed with a final appeal for conviction, "You ladies and gentlemen of this jury, today in these days of war, constitute the very front line of defense in this country. In behalf of the protection, the internal security of America and in that sense ladies and gentlemen, your government, my government, God forbid—Max Stephan's government, asks you to return a verdict of guilty as charged in this indictment."

After a five minute recess Judge Tuttle spoke to the jury. He explained the role of the various branches of the government—executive and judicial. He explained that it was then time for him to do his part, as it had been to preside at the trial. He explained that treason was the only crime specifically mentioned in the Constitution and he read from Article III, Section 3. In guiding the jury in their decision he went to great lengths to explain the point about aid to an individual as compared with aid to a country. He used the analogy of a corporation, telling the jury that no one person was a corporation. Neither, he said, was there a John Bull or an Uncle Sam, or a German equivalent of them who we must help in order to commit treason. Therefore, he explained, in order to help a country, we must help an individual. The point he was making was obvious. Later, someone wrote a pencilled note in the margin of the trial transcript alongside that part of Tuttle's charge to the jury. The note said, "directed verdict of guilty."

Tuttle went on to read the indictment and the overt acts, omitting the one that he had struck from the record. He explained the meaning of intent and reasonable doubt. He told the jury how to decide what evidence to consider and what not to consider. He said, "Now you go back to that woman whose testimony I struck out, which I ought not to do, but you remember I went after her a little. Now I knew when she got to where she wasn't telling the truth. I don't know why, but you have the right to common sense about those things." He was referring to Ludlow and her claim of never having been convicted. It was a strange comment that he made, however; one that could be used to justify the most irrational of decisions.

He explained that Stephan's not taking the stand should not be considered prejudicial, "that is his right," he said.

He concluded with the explanation that the sentence was his responsibility and that the jury must not give any consideration to the alternatives facing him.

Both Amberson and Lehr were asked if they had any exceptions and both answered, "No." It was then 4:15 on Thursday, July 2, and the jury was dismissed to consider its verdict.

Outside in the hallways, the show was on. There was an assortment of oddballs and curiosity seekers. One was "Irish Baron" John J. Hamly, who by his own statement was the last and only Irish Baron in existence. He was a resident of New York, was visiting in Windsor, and had been following the case in the eastern papers. He was dressed in a bright green tweed suit, its lapels covered with medals. One was a sheriff's badge. Thirteen year old Adolph Weinacker, a newspaper boy who had sold magazines to Stephan at the restaurant, was there to see his former customer. Young Adolph sagely told reporters, "He couldn't have known what he was doing."

In the jury room the first ballot was immediately taken. The vote was eleven for conviction and one for acquittal. Jerry Armstrong, the foreman, quickly identified himself as the lone dissenter, saying he had done so in order that they might at least have the opportunity to discuss the case. Another juror, Mrs. Marion B. Williams, later explained that the only discussion concerned whether or not Stephan intended to help the German government. She went on to explain that the jury seemed to be of the opinion that Stephan had plenty of time to decide what he was doing and that he did indeed intend to help Germany. The second ballot was unanimous for conviction.

At 5:35 P.M., after one hour and twenty minutes, there was a sharp knock on the jury room door. A bailiff took the message from Jerry Armstrong, "Tell the judge we have reached a verdict."

Stephan was two floors up in a special holding cage in the Federal Marshal's office. He and Agnes were talking in German to each other when the message came. They stopped and Max was led back to the courtroom. There was little doubt in his mind about the verdict. Back in the courtroom, during the routine before the jury was brought in, Stephan leaned over to Amberson and said, "I bet the verdict is guilty."

"You're right," said Amberson, "the verdict will be guilty."

Stephan told Amberson, "If the judge says I've got to hang, appeal the case."

The jury came back in and prepared for the formality of delivering its verdict. Judge Tuttle addressed them saying, "Ladies and gentlemen of the jury, have you agreed on a verdict?"

Jerry Armstrong, who was standing, replied, "We have."

Judge Tuttle said, "Do you find the defendant guilty or not guilty?"

The blood drained from Armstrong's face as he replied, "We find the defendant guilty as charged." Max Stephan turned red and blinked hard. Agnes turned to him and spoke rapidly in German.

The Clerk of the Court continued with the formalities. He said, "Ladies and gentlemen of the jury, hearken to your verdict as the court will record it. You say you find the defendant guilty in said indictment contained, and so say you all?"

The jury, standing, answered in unison, "We do."

Judge Tuttle then told the jury to be seated and complimented them on a just verdict. He credited the FBI and recognized the efforts of Amberson in defending Stephan. Of himself he said, "In these times people are likely to fill their hearts with hatred. I just tried to lean over backwards about it and felt it was my duty to do that." He then said that he would pass sentence in about a week. It was his practice, he explained, to get a report from the probation officer before sentencing. In deciding the sentence he said he wanted all the facts he could get on Stephan. Tuttle's week would become a month. The facts would prove damaging and would give Tuttle much of the justification for the harsh sentence he would deliver.

Stephan was taken back to the Federal Marshal's holding cage and two hours later was fast asleep and snoring. It was the evening of Thursday, July 2, and the trial that had begun on the previous Monday, was over.

Following the trial, Amberson was quoted as saying, "It seems to me that the FBI outsmarted Krug and got him to testify."

Both Lehr and Babcock praised the FBI for getting Krug to testify. Babcock said, "You have to give the FBI boys credit, they only asked Krug to tell the truth and he did that very well."

Several of the jury members commented also. Mr. Doensch said, "It takes all kinds to make a world, I've said what I think in the verdict."

Mrs. Ribble of Metamora, Michigan reflected on the possibility of condemning someone to death, but then she added that Stephan was helping Hitler and knew what he was doing. Another juror, Mrs. Carl, described the events when the first ballot was taken. She told of how relieved she was when Armstrong explained that he had cast the lone vote so that they could discuss the case. She said she felt better afterwards.

For Max Stephan, a long, agonizing countdown was only continuing.

Chapter 9

Court Resumes – The Sentencing

Ever since laws and punishments were defined, the convicted traitor could never expect a light sentence, nor has there ever been any attempt to rehabilitate the traitor. Generally, the intention has been to make an example of him, to influence the elements of society whose loyalty may be lacking and who might be contemplating a similar crime.

In treason punishments under old English law, the public was treated to something that was more of an anatomy lesson than anything else. The convicted traitor was first dragged to the gallows by a team of horses. He was then hanged slowly until he lost consciousness. Then he was revived, disemboweled, drawn and quartered, and beheaded. The remains were put on display in some central location and the offender's head frequently ended up on the top of a pike pole where his family could reclaim it weeks later, if they cared to. Few would contemplate treason under such conditions of punishment, and, of course, that was the whole idea.

By 1942 the more enlightened countries no longer staged bloody demonstrations in the town square. However, Judge Tuttle, operating in this more civilized environment, would do the best he could to serve up the necessary ingredients for the same deterrent. Furthermore, he would explain the sentence exactly that way, in so many words.

The Fourth of July, to which Babcock had so dramatically referred, was on a Saturday following the trial. On Monday, July 6, Prosecutor Lehr was to have another appointment in court. On that day he originally was scheduled to prosecute

Theodore Donay on the charge of misprision of treason. However, that trial was postponed and would not be held for almost a year. On that same Monday, Stephan was moved to the Federal Penitentiary at Milan, Michigan, 35 miles west of Detroit and just south of Ann Arbor. He became prisoner number 9565 and a little 3 × 5 card was typed, listing his name and date received. It also told why he was there, "TREASON—against the United States, awaiting sentence."

While that was happening the examination of Donay was beginning in earnest. On July 9, 1942, the FBI performed a "grilling" of him. Donay denied any knowledge of who Krug was or of giving him any money or help. He claimed that he first learned of Krug's identity in the papers. Of course, Krug's trial testimony had already refuted that. The FBI asked a number of questions that were phrased to test Donay's loyalty. These questions seem childish in retrospect but had a purpose at the time. Particularly, they asked him that if a German and American battleship were engaged in a battle, which one would he like to see win. Donay hedged. He said repeatedly that he would like to see the best ship win. He likened it to a duel in which he would want to see the best man win. The FBI, actually agents Earl Wynn and Harold Hove, asked him why a loyal, naturalized American citizen would not want the American ship to win. Donay had no real answer and gave the same type of answer in respect to a land battle. The agents asked Donay what he thought about the Nazi philosophy and Hitler's treatment of minorities in Germany. The question set off something in Donay. He alternatively stood up, paced the floor, and gestured while spewing a diatribe against the Jews. He expressed his belief that the American Government was dominated by Jews and that Hitler was right in exterminating "every damn Jew, down to the last one." He felt that America could not survive unless it followed the same policy as Hitler. As the interview went on Donay began to qualify his answers about who he wanted to win in a battle between German and American forces. He said that since the American ship would undoubtedly be the better one, then that would be the one he would want to win. Donay also took on a defense of Stephan, saying that Max was a good natured fellow and did not deserve to even be in jail, let alone charged with treason. He said that Stephan was a man who never had a serious thought in his mind and could hardly have done anything as serious as treason.

Donay accused the FBI of ruining his, Donay's, life, saying that he was being persecuted for his beliefs and that FBI policies were being dictated by Jews. Donay became incensed at any criticism of Hitler. He showed himself to be a man with intense hatred of the Jews. Anytime he talked on the subject he would stand and almost lose his composure. It must have been quite a spectacle for agents Wynn and Hove who probably could only shake their heads in disbelief when it was over.

Following the trial, an investigation into Stephan's past was begun by Chief U.S. Probation Officer Richard Doyle. Stephan's house of cards would begin to tumble when Doyle began delving into, among other things, the Windsor Police records. They contained the full documentation of the liquor law violations as well as the references to the "disorderly house." The dates of some of those violations gave the first indications of the falsified citizenship. It was readily admitted by Doyle that those facts had been available at the time Stephan applied for citizenship. However, it was explained that with 200 or so immigrants qualifying for citizenship each week it had been impossible to run complete checks on each. Usually only Detroit Police records were checked.

Tuttle had already expressed himself on the subject of a light sentence. He had duly noted that the minimum sentence of five years in prison would probably result in Stephan's simply being deported after the war.

Meanwhile the investigation was turning up the facts of more liquor license violations, the falsified residency for purposes of obtaining citizenship, and other damaging information.

During the month of July Stephan was quoted as saying that he was being made a "guinea pig." There was some indication of friction between lawyer and client and Amberson would soon be replaced.

Appearing in court to seek a new trial, Amberson said, "At the outset I want to make it clear that I never said I would not seek a new trial unless my client received the death penalty. This was Stephan's idea but the remarks were erroneously charged to me by the newspapers." He went on to claim that treason was possible only where aid and comfort to an enemy country was proved. In this case, he explained, the government's case was based on aid and comfort to an escaped flier. In what must certainly have been the weakest of his arguments he went on to explain that aid to an individual was not punishable as treason. Of course, Tuttle's charge to the jury had countered that point in the analogy of a corporation compared to a country. Since he had set forth his opinion earlier, Tuttle was predictably unmoved. He said, "But you did not object to the charge when it was given out."

Grasping at straws, Amberson replied, "No, the charge was correct but the jury did not follow the evidence." He went on to claim that the mention of Franz von Werra, the escapee who returned to Germany, was prejudicial.

The request for a new trial was denied on July 13th. On July 16th eviction proceedings were started by the owners of the restaurant. On July 17th Stephan had the first of two meetings that he was to have with Judge Tuttle, prior to the actual sentencing. The meeting on the 17th was at Stephan's request, so that he could tell "his side." Agnes was also present, along with a friend. Judge Tuttle allowed Stephan to say what he wanted.

Actually Agnes had seen Tuttle once prior to that meeting. She would meet with him once again at his request. Agnes was also busy bringing canned milk, fruit, candy, and other foods to Max at Milan, as she had done at the Wayne County Jail. Basic prison fare consisted of oatmeal, bread, and coffee.

On August 3 the readers of the Detroit Times were treated to a fairly typical form of reporting for those days. While the story had nothing to do with Stephan, it showed something of the form that newspaper reporting took during the war. On the front page of the Times that day was an almost full size photo of Japanese Premier Tojo's face. The caption under it was in quotes and said, "We will destroy the United States."

On August 4th Judge Tuttle requested that Max Stephan again meet with him. The purpose of that meeting was to present the mountain of unfavorable information that had been uncovered, so that Stephan might have a chance to explain away any part of it. Lawyers for both sides, as well as FBI agents were present. Tuttle became piqued because Stephan had not admitted any of the unsavory aspects of his past life until directly confronted with them.

On August 6th Judge Tuttle was ready to do what he had originally planned to do in a week. He had decided upon the sentence and had prepared a lengthy statement to precede it. Early that morning Max Stephan, with few doubts about what the sentence would be, was taken from the Milan Penitentiary for the trip to Judge Tuttle's court in Detroit. As with other trips, it was made by car in the custody of U.S. Marshals. During the ride Stephan became sick to his stomach and the car was stopped at the Rouge River bridge. Stephan threw up on the pavement, losing his false teeth. A Federal Marshal retrieved them, slightly chipped, and the party proceeded on their journey. They arrived at the court at 9 A.M. with an hour to wait.

Judge Tuttle was making his own preparations. He waved away photographers, telling them it was the most solemn day of his life. "I want nothing to interfere with the solemnity of this occasion," he said. In addition to this landmark case he was about to conclude, the day had another special meaning for him, although not the one he was referring to when he admonished the reporters. It was thirty years earlier, to the very day, that President Taft had appointed him to the Federal bench. The year had been 1912, and it was the same year in which Max Stephan had joined the Germany Army and launched himself on the sequence of events that would bring him there.

On his way to the courtroom Stephan was alternately optimistic and pessimistic. Reporters undoubtedly put some words in his mouth. One quote ran, "This war will soon be over and a victorious Germany will not leave Stephan in jail."

Nervously he said to Amberson, "Do you think the judge will hang me?" That was essentially the same question he had asked at the end of the trial, before he knew that sentencing was to be postponed. Consistently, Amberson gave the same answer he had given the last time, "Your guess is as good as mine."

Puffing on a "borrowed" cigar while being escorted to the courtroom, Stephan was quoted as saying, "Victory will be sure, Germany will not let me hang."

At 10 A.M. court convened and Judge Tuttle entered. He said, "This is the hour and the date set for the sentencing of Max Stephan." Stephan, standing before the judge was asked, "Is there anything you wish to say?"

Stephan said, "All I have to say is I am not guilty of treason for the reason I am not a traitor."

Tuttle replied, "I have already talked to you at length so you may be seated right there."

Stephan complied and Amberson told Judge Tuttle that he had tried to do his best. Judge Tuttle agreed, saying, "You did." He then began the reading of his statement, which in reality was an explanation for the sentence that he would deliver at its conclusion. The statement took 45 minutes to read and actually began with an explanation for its length.

Judge Tuttle discussed in great detail; his interviews with Max and Agnes Stephan, the investigation of Stephan's past, the lies on his General Motors application, Stephan's personal history and past law violations, his association with the Bund, Stephan's reputation for anti-American, pro-German statements, the loyalty of most German-Americans, the meeting between Krug and Mrs. Bertelmann, the aiding of Krug, further elaboration of the lies told by Stephan, Krug's escape and crossing of the Detroit River, conjecture that there could have been a plot involving the Sangers which was never proved, and finally a discussion of the overall fairness of the trial and jury.

Judge Tuttle then read the penalty for treason, "Whoever is convicted of treason shall suffer death; or at the discretion of the court, shall be imprisoned not less than five years and fined not less than $10,000, to be levied on and collected out of any of his property . . . "

Judge Tuttle then went into a lengthy discussion of the various reasons behind the penalties imposed on convicted criminals. He said, "At least three thoughts should always be in the minds of a court in imposing a criminal sentence. Of course the criminal law should be enforced and sentences imposed which will be just to the offender, on one hand, and also just to society on the other hand."

He went on to explain that there were cases where light sentences were appropriate. Those were instances when, for example, young offenders simply had to be taught a lesson. He explained, "it needs no statements from this court to show that this is not that kind of case . . . "

Next he described the situation in which it is not reasonable to expect to reform the offender and the objective of the sentence is to put the criminal away for as long as possible so as to not do any further harm to society. He then explained that a sentence like that would fall short of the duty of the court in this case.

Then he explained the situation, as he saw it, in the case of Max Stephan, "There is a third reason for enforcing the criminal law and imposing sentence which is sometimes present and which I think is present right now in a large measure and is the one that ought to be controlling in fixing the sentence. This goes far beyond seeing to it that Max Stephan does not again commit treason; it has to do with others in our country who, like Max Stephan, are citizens of our country, but at heart are disloyal to our country and at heart love the enemy better than they do the cause of the United States and want the Axis to win this war."

"This court would fall short of doing its duty if it did not by this sentence teach a lesson to every disloyal citizen who would like to adhere to the enemy and aid and assist the enemy during this awful war. Will a five year sentence teach that lesson to the disloyal citizens of the United States? Does this need an answer? Let us go on up to imprisonment for life—will that teach the lesson to the disloyal citizens of the United States?

It was said that in the courtroom people formed the word "No" with their lips in a silent response to Tuttle's roll call of alternatives.

"This court has considered that question very seriously. In order to answer that question it is necessary to know what a life sentence means. It, of course, may mean that the party will stay in prison so long as he lives. In actual fact it does not very often mean that, because under the statutes of the United States a defendant sentenced to life is eligible to parole at the end of 15 years. More than that, it is well known from the history of this country that after a war is over, or within a few years thereafter, most people who are in prison for some offense growing out of the war either are paroled or their sentences are commuted, or in some way they are released. This court is not the only one who knows that. These disloyal citizens know this better than our good loyal citizens do. In other words, any imprisonment imposed by this court is discounted by every disloyal citizen who contemplates aid to the enemy. There is no way this court can fool them about it and make them think that a life sentence means staying in prison until the party dies. They know better than that. So this court asks itself, will a sentence which by parole may be shortened to 15 years serve as a sufficient deterrent to this disloyal element? It seems actually plain that a negative answer is required. Then this court asks itself, will a sentence of death be a greater deterrent to these fifth columnists? It seems to this court that there is only one answer to that question and it is in the affirmative. It is, of course, a dreadful thing to take a human life, but we must remember that the offense of treason has to do with war, and we must remember that war has to do with death. The life of this traitor, Max Stephan, is less valuable than the lives of our loyal sons, which are being given to the cause of the United States. We have been soft, to the extent of being mushy. There are too many in the sob squad and too few in the fighting squad. This is no ordinary war. We talk of soldiers and think of death not in figures of thousands, but in figures of millions. If the lives of many of our boys are to be taken to help such a cause, this court should not hesitate to take the life of one traitor if it, in turn, will help that same just cause. This court should, in no hesitating or uncertain way, say to the disloyal element that during this awful war the penalty for treason is death."

That was the conclusion of the statement, although for all practical purposes, the sentence had been delivered. All that was left was the official pronouncement, phrased in language so formal that Agnes Stephan would not really know what had happened until someone explained it to her. It was required that Max Stephan stand while it was recited.

Judge Tuttle continued, "On this August 6, 1942, came the United States Attorney . . . "

" . . . It is by the court ordered and adjudged, and the court does now here sentence this defendant, that this defendant, Max Stephan, be remanded to the custody of the United States Marshal for the Eastern District of Michigan, and be by him taken to the Federal Correctional Institution at Milan, Michigan, and there confined in safe and secure custody until November 13, 1942, and on that day, within the walls of the Federal Correctional Institution or within an enclosed yard thereof the said defendant, Max Stephan, be by the said United States Marshal hanged by the neck until he, the said Max Stephan, is dead."

One lone handclap, instantly silenced, was heard coming from the back of the courtroom. Then there was a minor disturbance at the door to the courtroom involving some people who were trying to get in.

Judge Tuttle, borrowing a lesson from old English law, had at least been brutally honest in his reasons. There was no question that Stephan was being condemned to death to serve as an example to others. The execution date, November 13th was, dramatically, a Friday and seemed to further emphasize the point.

Stephan, his hands over his face, was rushed from the courtroom. He kept saying, "They'll never hang me, they'll never hang me," while being taken to the elevator through a path cleared by waiting Marshals. Judge Tuttle, his duty done, left the court for a dental appointment. Prosecutor Lehr had no comment.

Agnes Stephan, who had not understood the formally phrased pronouncement, was frantically trying to find out what had happened. She muttered to a court attendant, "What, you mean?"

"Yes," she was told.

"I want my Max."

She was on the verge of fainting and court employes attended to her for 45 minutes before bringing her under control. She had no friends or relatives with her to help. It was said that her closest relative in the U.S. was a nun in California. A U.S. Marshal took her in a taxi to the home of a German doctor on East Grand Boulevard. A neighbor came out and said, 'Today is the doctor's day off." She decided to walk for a while and Jane Schermerhorn, earlier writer of feature articles on Krug, tagged along. Agnes reminisced about their chow, Arnold, and told of the restaurant being padlocked. She said she now had a room with a family where she worked as a housekeeper. She repeated the same theme that Max had recited, that he had done what any American would have done if the situation had been reversed. This gained little sympathy since the Nazi reputation for ruthlessness was well documented.

In fact, had the situation been fully reversed, an American Max Stephan in Germany would have been beheaded by an executioner dressed in evening clothes and a mask. Hitler was responsible for the ritual details. He felt that beheading was more Teutonic than hanging, shooting, or electrocuting.

Agnes and Schermerhorn stopped at a restaurant for coffee and Agnes rambled on. She described the plight of post-World War I Germany, attributing World War II to those conditions. She was at least correct to the point that those conditions made it possible for Hitler to gain power. She said that the people in her native Cologne were left crippled and hopeless and "crazily revolted against the world." She told of the Moroccan occupation troops, men never noted for their kindness or compassion, swinging whips at people during the post-World War I occupation of the Rhineland. She described the bombing of Cologne in World War I, as she remembered it from her girlhood. In a Teutonic obsession with death, gory detail, and graphic description, she told of the fate of two "beautiful flaxen haired girls" who were working in a department store during an air raid. The store was hit and, as she put it, afterwards the firemen washed what was left of them off the walls. She described the FBI as wicked men.

Amberson, in full retreat, was quoted as saying that a lawyer sells his services, not himself.

Inasmuch as the sentencing was in the morning of August 6th, the story could still make the papers on that day. The Detroit Times, in three inch headlines, simply said;

STEPHAN TO HANG

The usually more objective Detroit News used both upper and lower case letters to announce:

Stephan Doomed to Hang as a Traitor
Execution set for Nov. 13 at Milan

However, the News departed from its usual objectivity in one of its three front page articles on the case, which started, "Pig-faced Max Stephan. . . . "

By the next day Stephan was saying, "I'll appeal. What I did was just a misdemeanor, not treason. I won't hang. That sentence was dictated by Washington. I should have gotten about ten years. The war will be over soon and then Germany and America can lick hell out of the Japs." The reference to Washington was erroneous and, as will be seen, many highly placed officials in Washington really felt that the death sentence was too severe. Stephan's reference to Germany and America "licking" the Japs was, of course, ludicrous and shows that Stephan was not a man of even average intellect. However, it does reflect one thought at the time. The course of the war was not going well and it was not all that clear at the time that Germany would be beaten. The earlier quotes attributed to Stephan indicated that he hoped to stall for as long as possible so that he might be saved by a German victory.

On August 7th the Detroit Free Press printed the results of interviews with 17 Detroiters, one a minister, chosen at random on the street. They were asked to assess Stephan's death penalty. All 17 agreed with the sentence. "He got what he deserved," was the most quoted remark, however, several concluded their interviews noting that the death penalty was, "a little harsh." They were caught in the same trap as many of the judges who would review the case; to show mercy was to show weakness and no one wanted that label in wartime.

August 7th continued to be a good news day. Also surfacing was G. Phil Hanna, referred to as America's number one hangman. Hanging, apparently, was more like a hobby than a full time profession for the grisly Hanna. On a full time basis he was a farmer in Illinois. It was he who was said to have hanged Chebatoris following Tuttle's sentence in 1938. Seventy others before Chebatoris had also received Hanna's ministrations, so he was no rank amateur. Actually, he did not charge for his services, but instead donated his time out of sympathy. He claimed to have achieved skill at his sideline and believed that in doing it efficiently he was actually performing a humane act. Amateurs caused needless suffering, he said, as he volunteered to hang Stephan. Actually, U.S. Marshal John J. Barc was in charge of the hanging. He could use the services of Hanna as he saw fit. Barc would supervise the building of the gallows and was responsible for the effective carrying out of the sentence.

Filling the 7th of August with further details was William Zack, another feature writer for the Detroit Times. He performed six hours worth of research on the crime of treason and reported the results. He said that if Stephan were to hang, he would be the second person to die for treason. There had been previous treason trials and convictions, including a notable case resulting from the Whisky Rebellion in 1795. At that time, Pennsylvania farmers were enraged over the Federal taxes on the whisky they made. They considered the manufacture of whisky to be a God-given right. John Mitchell and Hans Vigel were convicted and sentenced to death but President Washington intervened.

If Stephan would indeed be the second to die, the first was a New Orleans gambler by the name of William Mumford, claimed Zack. Mumford had refused to recognize the Federal occupation of his native city in 1862. To emphasize his point he tore a U.S. flag from a pole and dragged it through the streets. He was executed by a firing squad and would probably not be consoled by the fact that a little over a hundred years later acts similar to his would be performed regularly and without punishment on the streets of many U.S. cities. Of course, Mumford was tried by a Military Court and may not have been comparable to Stephan.

Another event on the 7th of August was Judge Tuttle's interview with the press. He had granted it so that they might be even better informed about the famous case just concluded. Some of the reporters arrived early and found the Judge in a talkative mood. He was smoking his corncob pipe as he greeted the early arrivals. Sitting in his shirt-sleeves, he chatted about hunting and fishing, then, as now, good subjects in Michigan in any gathering of men. On his shirt was a small Sigma Alpha Epsilon fraternity pin. Judge Tittle had been founder of the University of Michigan Chapter of that fraternity and had once been the national director.

At the appointed hour he put on his coat and an attendant brought a stack of telegrams to him. All, of course, were strongly in support of his sentence. As he read them he broke into tears. He went on to disclose how he had been under guard for the past 35 days in case anyone might try to harm him and stop the sentencing.

On that same day another major news story was coming to a conclusion. Eight Nazi saboteurs had previously been captured and six of them were to die the next day in a Washington, D.C. electric chair. The eight were German spies, landed on eastern beaches from submarines. The FBI had tapped into their wireless communication system and was practically waiting for them on the beaches when they landed. Originally all eight were to be executed, however two of them had decided to provide the Government with information and their lives were to be spared. The executions were carried out on schedule and the comparison of the crimes and sentences was mentioned during Stephan's appeal.

Stephan's sentence was ominous news back in Canadian POW camps. Of course, one prisoner, Peter Krug, had a direct personal concern in the case and felt more deeply about it than the others. In August he was no longer at Bowmanville. The "top escapers," himself included, had been moved to the "escape proof" camp at Gravenhurst, the recently completed site of "the most beautiful fence in Canada." "Doc" Wagner, Walter Manhart, Ulrich Steinhilper, Pfundtner, and other Bowmanville "bad boys" were there.

Krug's feeling of concern went beyond Stephan, who he knew was largely his own victim. Krug was probably more concerned for the future of others he had brought to harm, primarily Mrs. Bertelmann. It still bothered him that he had gone to her, not even knowing her or if she would help, and had caused her to be put in a detention camp.

Meanwhile Stephan was back in Milan Penitentiary. His little 3 × 5 card now had a new notation on it, "Aug. 6, Ret. from US Dist. Court under sentence, death."

Chapter 10

Appeal

If war hysteria was a factor in Stephan's sentence, it would be no less of a factor during the appeals. The latter half of 1942 would bring the Allies little cause for optimism. The admirals and generals who had predicted victory over Japan in 90 days were, by then, clearly wrong. Even a fourteen year old, such as myself at the time, could see that we were fighting enemies of considerable strength. All we had to do was look at the maps that we had pinned to our walls.

Furthermore, there appeared to be more spies and saboteurs loose among us, as evidenced by an August 10th newspaper story. We were told on that date that in the East a field had been plowed to form an arrow pointing to an airfield. In another case, grain was stacked so as to point to an airplane factory. It now seemed that the enemy was preparing to attack mainland America. One could wonder, if Krug had gotten away, would he be preparing to follow those pointers?

On August 19th Detroiters received news of a British defeat that struck close to home. It had ramifications that would reach back to the German prisoners in Canada and to Gravenhurst and Bowmanville. August 19, 1942 was the date of the Dieppe raid—an attack launched to test German defenses on the Normandy coast. The attacking force was primarily Canadian and only a third of them returned. The rest were either killed or taken prisoner. The disaster was magnified in Windsor because of the Canadian and British custom of having their military units represent specific geographic areas. One unit in the raid was the Essex Scots from Windsor. The

Detroit papers carried the detailed casualty lists, name by name. There was considerable anxiety over the missing, until later when prisoner lists became available and were printed. The ramifications dealt with the treatment of prisoners. Earlier the British had raided certain channel islands held by the Germans and had put prisoners in chains during those raids, so one version went. Hitler was enraged when he received word of that, and retaliated by putting Dieppe prisoners in chains or shackles. Thus a shackling escalation was begun. Word was sent out to the prison camps across Canada. At each camp, administrators were to put a given number of prisoners in shackles. At Bowmanville, Otto Kretschmar led the prisoners in resistance to the order. Troops were called in and fire hoses were used. The prisoners were finally forced to submit and 100 of them, the Bowmanville allotment, were placed in shackles. At Gravenhurst the prisoners resisted by repeatedly unlocking the shackles and freeing themselves. Later, word was received that the chains had been removed from the prisoners held in Germany and the chapter was closed.[2]

Meanwhile, the Stephan's appeal had started. It was up to Agnes, who probably possessed 75% of the couple's combined brain power, to get the process moving. With the sentencing over and done with, it was clear to her, and to Max, that a new lawyer was needed.

Actually, with help from a friend, Agnes had begun to look for a new lawyer within a week after the trial. The friend was Anders J. Hammelef, the man who, in cooperation with the beer coil cleaner, had warned Max about his German sympathies earlier.

Following the trial, but before the sentencing, Agnes was staying with friends. At that time she called Hammelef and the two visited Amberson. Hammelef did not like Amberson and told Agnes that she should find someone else. Within a short time he suggested another lawyer who, it turned out, had been suggested to Agnes by others. He was Nicholas Salowich, a 47 year old Detroiter who had a reputation, which he disclaimed, as a criminal lawyer. It was a reputation that had been earned in 1930 and 1931 when he had been one of the defense lawyers in the so-called Jerry Buckley murder case, a famous Detroit trial that put Salowich's face on the front pages of the papers.

The Buckley case had been a classic, prohibition era, gangland slaying. Jerry Buckley had been a popular radio announcer who had been outspoken in his criticism of Detroit Mayor Charles Bowles. In July of 1930 a recall election was successful in removing Bowles from office. Within hours Buckley was lured to the lobby of the LaSalle Hotel by a mystery woman. There, while reading a paper, he was shot eleven times, or in the parlance of the papers, he received eleven slugs to the head and body. All sorts of allegations flew. Some said that the mob was after him for other things, and the murder was committed after the Bowles recall to make it look like that was the reason. Others were outspoken in claiming a link with the recall. Three men were accused of the crime, Joe Bommarito, Ted Pizzini, and Angelo Livecchi. Pizzini was arrested in New York City and had to be extradited to Michigan. Then New York Governor, Franklin Roosevelt signed the extradition papers. The prosecution called over 100 witnesses, including the "Negro" porter who was alleged to have seen one of the men tiptoe up behind Buckley. The hotel detective testified, along with a taxi driver and a host of others. The defense had witnesses that placed at least one of the accused in New York at the time of the killing. All three had to be found guilty or all three would be innocent. On April 22, 1931 the jury found them "not guilty." The names associated with the case, or appearing in the paper at the same time, read like something from a Damon Runyon short story. There was "Black Leo", "Stuttering Harry" Sominsky, and "Yosher" Kaplan, to name just a few.

Salowich, though born in Wilkes-Barre, Pennsylvania, was nevertheless a native Detroiter, having received his higher education at the University of Detroit and having lived in the city for many years. In the First World War he had been a Lieutenant in the Tank Corps and was justifiably proud of his record.

He was the oldest son in a distinguished family that had emigrated to the U.S. from Galicia. Geographically, Galicia is a heterogeneous area located approximately where Poland,

The Ukraine, and Czechoslovakia all meet on our present maps. Virtually every country around Galicia has at one time or another embraced it within its borders. The people consist of Poles, Czechs, and Germans, as well as Ukrainians. Some people thought that Salowich was Jewish, a fact that would have been ironic in view of his defense of Stephan. Salowich occasionally perpetuated the myth of his Jewishness in offhand remarks. In fact, he was of the Russian Orthodox faith and was an officer in the Church of Ss. Peter and Paul.

In addition to his church membership, Salowich was active in the Kiwanis and the American Legion. He loved those kinds of organizations and the friends he made there. At one time his wife had insisted on joining the Yacht Club. Salowich did, but was unhappy there and felt totally out of place. He simply could not relate to the people.

When Agnes came to him he was not lacking in knowledge of the case. He had, for years, been the lawyer for Theodore Donay and would be representing him in the case that was now being brought against him in connection with Stephan and Krug. Donay's trial, scheduled for the week after Stephan's, had been delayed and would not be held until May, 1943. Donay, incidentally, was also in the Milan Federal Prison.

Salowich had attended part of Stephan's trial because of the link between it and Donay. He had been enraged over the appearance and testimony of Krug, Nazi salute and all, which he had witnessed. For Salowich, that had been a preview because later when Donay came up for trial, Krug would be back, seemingly to haunt him, he thought.

Salowich told Mrs. Stephan that he would take the case but that his fee would be $10,000. She agreed, although the couple was virtually penniless at the time. With no money actually having been received, Salowich entered the case along with Amberson who was still the attorney of record. Meanwhile, Mrs. Stephan set out to try to raise the money.

She had at least found a lawyer who was not afraid to hold and express a personal conviction about the case. Salowich truly believed that Max Stephan's crime was not treason. He felt that the charge should have been the lesser one of harboring an enemy alien. Furthermore, on a purely personal basis he wanted to go down in legal history as the man who had gotten a definition of treason from the Supreme Court, a definition that he felt was totally lacking.

Actually, people who did not feel Stephan should hang were divided into two camps. There were those who felt as Salowich did and there were those who felt that the crime was indeed treason but that death was too severe a punishment for Stephan's brand of it. This latter group could cite the minimum penalty of five years as evidence that somewhere, someone had recognized various severities of the crime.

Salowich had a partner by the name of McCabe who was something of a character, although a highly educated one. In addition to being an attorney, he was a medical doctor, a geologist, a petroleum engineer and held, or had held, professorships at two southern universities. Unfortunately he was incapable of earning money at anything and lived like a sea lamphrey on those around him. His problem seemed to be that he was incapable of completing anything. He was easily recognizable by his cowboy boots and modified western hat. He lived in the Salowich house, even having his son with him, from time to time, and almost steadily through the Stephan appeal.

Salowich had a son, Nicholas, Jr., who was fourteen years old at the time of the appeal. He and his father played cribbage together; it was their shared time together. Young Nicholas recalled his irritation and resentment when McCabe, while living in their home, would actually interrupt those games to discuss some point in the Stephan case.

McCabe would do much of the research for the case, a job for which he was ideally suited. He readily produced reams of copious notes, carefully written on legal sized yellow paper. The pages would include the study of cases such as the Aaron Burr treason trial of 1806. In that particular case, Burr, whose aims were obscure, was thought to have been attempting to set up a separate country in the southwest. He was found not guilty of an overt act of treason. The Constitutional requirement for two witnesses may have been what saved him.

That same Constitutional requirement may have been a factor in a potential treason case during the Vietnam War. The American movie actress, Jane Fonda, went to Hanoi, the capitol city of our enemy, the North Vietnamese. While there she posed for pictures, was videotaped at an anti-aircraft gun, broadcast radio speeches aimed at encouraging American servicemen to abandon their duties, and generally hobnobbed with officials. Surely, it was "aid and comfort to the enemy" and might well have been a treasonous act. However, while millions saw her on tape and heard her speeches, two witnesses who actually saw her do those acts would probably have had to testify at a trial. Of course, the country was bitterly divided on the whole issue of that war and it is doubtful if the Government even cared to make a martyr of a movie actress, which certainly they would have done.

Salowich and Tuttle were to be at sword's point much of the time and the two seemed to have a mutual dislike for each other. Undoubtedly Tuttle regarded Salowich as a man who set criminals free, a thorn in his side. In later years Salowich related an incident, far removed from the case, that involved himself and Judge Tuttle. He was walking down Woodward Avenue, Detroit's main street, during a parade or festival. He ran into Tuttle who was carrying an old muzzle loading rifle. Salowich was surprised and asked the Judge what he was doing. Tuttle replied that he always carried the musket, a family heirloom, each year in that particular festival. A Federal Judge carrying a musket on Woodward Avenue was as foreign to Salowich as Galicia was to Tuttle.

Salowich's main tactic and contribution was to fight a delaying action, winning first one postponement of the execution and then another. Tuttle, on the other hand, fought each delay with all the machinery he had at hand. It was said by some that he was as bent on hanging Stephan as he had been with Chebatoris. In any event, Salowich knew that he had another adversary, war hysteria, and it was stronger than all the others.

The appeal process was started by Amberson on August 13th when he filed a Notice of Appeal to the Circuit Court. In the labyrinth of legal routine, it was then necessary to file a so-called assignment of error, an account of the trial flaws that supported the appeal. On September 2nd, Salowich, Amberson, Lehr, and Babcock met in Tuttle's courtroom to discuss the appeal. Salowich requested a thirty day extension in which to file the Assignment of Error. Tuttle refused the request, saying that if it looked like the job would take so long, maybe there really were no errors, maybe Salowich was just trying to stall. Salowich said, "The indictment is as faulty and as full of holes as a swiss cheese." By the 5th of September Amberson was out of the case. On the 8th of September the Assignment of Error had still not been filed and everyone was back in court listening to Salowich's reasons for the delay. In reply to Tuttle, Salowich explained that it would take a few more days. One of the reasons he gave was that he had to appear in another case, before another judge. The case happened to be the revocation of Mrs. Stephan's citizenship, which he was handling for Agnes. Tuttle was unsympathetic, telling Salowich that he shouldn't have taken another case if there was a scheduling difficulty. Nevertheless, on Thursday, September 10th, Salowich presented the Assignment of Error. Twenty-five specific points were listed, including;

> The overt acts did not support treason.
>
> The indictment was faulty.
>
> The Court erred in letting a sworn enemy of the U.S. testify as a competent witness.
>
> Krug was in uniform.
>
> The Court did not compel Krug to answer on cross-examination, therefore his testimony should have been stricken.
>
> The Court should have struck Krug's testimony on the grounds that he had been misled, misinformed, and tricked into believing that he was correcting a wrong he had committed.

Krug was guilty of forgery and theft.

Witnesses were led.

Testimony failed to prove an overt act of treason.

The Court erred in denying a directed verdict.

The Court allowed Lehr to inflame the jury.

The charge did not clearly define the aim of treason.

The Court did not instruct the jury on what constituted an overt act.

Use of words "spy," "secret agent," and "secret agent of German Government" were prejudicial.

With the basis for the appeal defined, the next step, on the 10th of September, was to take the formal appeal to a printer in preparation for going to the Circuit Court of Appeals. The cost of the printing was to be shared and Tuttle admonished Salowich to make a good bargain. Salowich said, "Your honor, my Jewish instincts will prompt me to do just that."

Meanwhile, in addition to the problems with the revocation of citizenship, Mrs. Stephan was having other problems. No one wanted to loan or give her any money. She had gone to all the clubs and organizations with which she and Max had been associated and had been turned down, possibly with a few anonymous exceptions. When the appeal was prepared and ready, she paid Salowich $2,500. It was all the money he ever received and it did not even cover his expenses, which among other things, included at least one trip to Washington. As to where the $2,500 came from, little is known. Hammelef, probably the couple's only friend, had made a sincere effort to raise money. He had approached the various German organizations as well as some individuals. Finally he had to stop. He received several anonymous phone threats and simply did not care to go on with the effort. He probably succeeded in raising a small amount of money which may have been combined with what Agnes raised and the last of the couple's savings, but no donors cared to have their names mentioned publicly.

Salowich was also suffering from the association with Stephan. He had become known as the "traitor's lawyer" and would spend a year of his life on the receiving end of insults from former friends and others. Even his mother once said to him, "Nicholas, if it's money you need . . . " Salowich easily ignored the insults. Unfortunately it was having a traumatic effect on his family. The center of their community was around Livernois and Fenkell in Detroit which was an area consisting primarily of eastern European immigrants. While a diverse group, they shared a common hatred for the Germans and the Nazis, who, even at the time of Stephan's appeal, were burning and brutalizing their native lands and probably relatives who had not been fortunate enough to leave. Salowich family members were accused of being "Nazi lovers." They received threatening letters and phone calls and, in general, went through an unpleasant period in their lives. There was even one falling-out within the family.

While enduring all that, Salowich, had a deep personal dislike for Stephan. He referred to him as a "pig" and used other derogatory words when talking about him. While having some personal motivations for taking the case, it is certain that those motivations were little reward, compared to the abuse. He stayed with Stephan simply because he believed in what he was doing; he was seeing that Stephan got a fair shake in the legal system.

Out at Milan the necessary preparations for the hanging were being made. Rope and lumber had been ordered. They were both critical wartime materials and a special priority was required to buy them. Ninety five feet of 3/4 inch, 5,400 pound test rope was purchased. A gallows was constructed. That was a two week job and it was built in sections so that it could be easily and quickly brought out, assembled and disassembled. The hanging was to be done well before dawn on the appointed day so as to have as little effect as possible on the other prisoners who were expected to be restless. Also, it was not desirable to interfere with the normal working schedule at the prison.

In general, prison personnel were correct, and even on occasion, sympathetic toward Stephan. However, some guards did resort to cruelty by constantly reminding him that he would soon hang. They were cool but courteously correct toward Salowich and he did not learn until later of the cruelty of some. Warden Shuttlesworth appeared sympathetic throughout.

On September 26th Agnes Stephan's citizenship was revoked. Since Max's conviction she had stayed first with one friend, and then another, and finally she was living in a room at the home of Erna Schwartz, the former waitress at the restaurant. When the revocation of citizenship was completed she was interned in a camp for dangerous enemy aliens for the duration of the war.

On October 5th, with the execution date still firm, another would-be hangman offered his services. A certain Irving Greenberg had called the Detroit Times and the editor apparently saw fit to print his picture and story on the front page. Admittedly lacking in experience, he felt that he could contribute a great deal of enthusiasm. He was quoted, "I'll be able to go to bed that night with a clear conscience. One less Nazi means my home is that much safer."

By October 13th President Roosevelt had several letters in his "Max Stephan" file. On that date he received a wire from a New York woman asserting that an injustice had been done to Max Stephan. She praised him for loving his fatherland and quoted at length from the scriptures. Her message was filed away with an August 7th wire from an Iowa citizens group demanding a speedy execution.

An appeal from Tuttle's District Court went to the U.S. Circuit Court of Appeals in Cincinnati. That court is a six judge panel, at least five of whom must hear any given case. By early November it was clear that the appeal would not be heard prior to the scheduled execution date, and on November 7th a stay of execution was issued.

On December 12th the case was submitted and argued before the Appeals Court. Nagel was asked to give a statement in reference to the restaurant incident. In it he admitted being in the restaurant but denied any conversation about Krug.

Stephan's case was argued by Salowich. Babcock, the prosecutor from the original trial, argued for the Government. Salowich presented several points that seemed to be of interest to the Judges. One important point was that the only charge that truly related to treason, the buying of the bus ticket for Krug, was not witnessed by two persons, the Constitutional requirement for treason. Also, Salowich pressed the point that Krug had refused to answer questions on cross-examination. This, said Salowich, had deprived his client of due process of law. The Court seemed to be particularly interested in that point. Salowich claimed that, as an admitted forger, Krug was ineligible to testify in court. The whole issue of Krug's testimony and appearance was a major issue with Salowich, including presentation of the gun, Krug's uniform, and everything relating to him. Salowich also argued the point of excessive penalty, claiming that it was the investigation that influenced the death penalty and much of that information was not available in court for cross-examination.

On December 12, 1943 the Appeals Court gave its ruling, upholding Judge Tuttle and the trial proceedings. One of the judges told Salowich privately that they never had any intention of doing otherwise because they wanted the case to go to the Supreme Court. The appeal had done nothing more than buy time for Stephan, but for him, that was enough.

On March 4th, with the stay of execution still in effect, the case was filed with the Supreme Court. The appeal cited the Nagel issue and the question of citizenship. Salowich went to Washington in preparation for arguing the case before the Supreme Court. He found that four of the Justices were sympathetic to some form of reduced sentence. Three of the four were known to have been Murphy, Jackson, and Stone, the Chief Justice. However, Stone indicated to Salowich that there looked like little chance of any of the other five Justices swinging over. Stone advised Salowich to go and see Attorney General Biddle and see what he might do. Salowich went to Biddle's office and was kept waiting for what he felt was an excessively long time. Finally Biddle, in Salowich's words, literally bounced out of his office saying something to the effect, "I'll give you two minutes to tell me why Stephan shouldn't hang." Salowich was infuriated by Biddle's pompous display and started to leave. Biddle called him back and the two sat down for 45 minutes to discuss the case. But it was to no avail.

Back in Detroit, on March 31st, August Marquette, a photographer for the Detroit Times, won a $50 prize for the photo he had taken back on August 6, 1942, of Max Stephan leaving the courtroom after being sentenced to death. The picture was reprinted.

On April 5th, 1943, the Supreme Court delivered its opinion on the case. The appeal was denied on the basis that the trial contained no reversible error. The Detroit Times carried a three inch headline saying;

STEPHAN MUST DIE

Supreme Court Rules

April 14th was the date set for Stephan to return to Tuttle's court for resentencing.

On April 10th Stephan wrote a letter to Supreme Court Justice Frank Murphy, the Justice who was reportedly a friend of Nagel's. When Murphy had been Governor of Michigan from 1936 to 1938 he had won nationwide praise for his handling of the 1937 sit-down strikes in the auto plants, primarily in Flint, Michigan. However he had not been reelected. A loyal New Deal Democrat, he had then been appointed Attorney General and was, in fact, Biddle's predecessor. He had been appointed to the Supreme Court on January 3, 1940. Stephan, in his letter to him, continued to press the point about Nagel, claiming that he, Stephan, could have had Nagel testify, but did not, for the reasons described earlier—Nagel would help in the background.

Murphy wrote back advising him to write to Judge Tuttle and ask for a new trial on the basis of new evidence.

Before Murphy's reply was received, however, Stephan was having other problems. On April 12th it was reported that he was under the care of a doctor. A headline said;

Stephan breaks down in death cell

Back before the Supreme Court ruling he had joked, "I'm going to demand a silk robe." Now he begged visitors, "Tell the judge I didn't mean any harm." Actually his visitors were few. Agnes had been sent to the internment camp in Texas, and Salowich was one of his few contacts.

Another was the Reverend C.E. Ferguson, Chaplain and Pastor of the Free Methodist Church of Milan. When asked if Stephan was a religious man he said, "No, I can't say that he is, but he does seem to get some consolation out of the scriptures." Of course, none of Stephan's friends wanted to be linked with him in any way, not even by a simple visit at the prison.

Stephan never understood why Krug testified and must have cursed him a thousand times. In a conversation with Salowich he referred to the *Oberleutnant* as "the dog that bites the hand that feeds him."

On April 13th, the day before the resentencing, Salowich said that he had abandoned further court fights. He claimed to have requested the necessary forms for direct appeal to the President.

On April 14th Stephan was again brought before Judge Tuttle. Once again hundreds of spectators were gathered in the halls to see him. There was even a Canadian soldier who was using leave time just to see Stephan. He was brought into the courtroom just as the clock began to strike 10 A.M. On the last gong, Judge Tuttle entered. Stephan was kept in handcuffs, which despite pleas, Tuttle refused to have removed. It meant that Stephan also had to keep his overcoat on throughout the proceedings. He sat in his place quietly sobbing. Court opened with the traditional, "Hear ye, hear ye, God bless the United States of America and this honorable Court."

Salowich was late in arriving for reasons that had previously been explained to the court. McCabe, Salowich's partner, was there in his place wearing his usual cowboy boots. When Salowich finally entered late, he went directly to the table where Stephan sat and said, "Come on, cheer up." Stephan grabbed his hands.

Judge Tuttle then read a statement in preparation for the resentencing. He emphasized each word with his forefinger, something he seldom did, as his nasal voice droned on. Occasionally he spread his arms out, giving a bat like appearance in his judicial robes. Salowich sought a delay at least until mid-May, pleading the nearness of Holy Week and Easter. Tuttle answered, "The only time I'll permit is time for the respondent to make peace with his maker. I do not want to allow additional time in which he would only suffer."

With that, the execution was set for April 27th, not far away, and Stephan was returned to Milan. However, that date did not stand for long. On April 16th a stay of execution was again issued by the Supreme Court, this time so that an appeal for a new trial could be prepared. Salowich would not yet abandon further court fights as he said he would do.

On April 17th Stephan wrote his letter to Judge Tuttle at Murphy's suggestion, asking for a new trial. The letter was hand printed on cheap, lined tablet paper and again dwelt on the Nagel issue. The date of the letter was one day short of a year since the Nagel incident, real or imaginary, had occurred.

Salowich entered the formal appeal for a new trial on April 28th. He gave as reasons, the Nagel incident and the fact that the jury had not been secluded.

The question of whether Nagel was involved was becoming a larger issue. Stephan continued to claim that his conversation with Nagel, he felt, satisfied one requirement of the law in that Nagel should qualify as a Government official, and therefore no concealment was involved. That argument, naturally enough, carried little weight.

In any event, on April 30th Nagel was called by the FBI for further and more detailed questioning. He brought his lawyer, John Dohrman, with him. In the interview, actually a deposition, Nagel again denied any discussion concerning Krug. He told of seeing Mrs. Stephan several times after the arrest. The first conversation, he said, was to advise her on how to sell or dispose of some restaurant equipment. In a second conversation with her he claimed she asked him for advice regarding an attorney to replace Amberson. She had apparently asked Mr. Hammelef for similar advice at about the same time. Nagel claimed that he recommended "a high grade fellow like Tom Chawk." Whoever he was, he did not become the chosen one.

Nagel mentioned that sometime after that he received a call from Nicholas Salowich who requested that he come to his office. Nagel went and took Dohrman, his lawyer, with him. Apparently Salowich showed Nagel a letter from Stephan describing the alleged restaurant conversation. Nagel told Salowich that it was a "pack of damn lies." Nagel claimed, still in the FBI interview, that Salowich then asked him for some assistance on an appeal to the President through Frank Murphy, Nagel's friend and Supreme Court Justice. Nagel declined the request and felt that he was also being very gently asked for financial help but admitted that no direct request for money was made at that time.

Nagel told the FBI that he only heard from Salowich one more time. About a week after the meeting, he came home one afternoon and had a message from his daughter to call Salowich. He turned the matter over to Dohrman who made the call. Dohrman told the FBI that Salowich made a direct appeal for money. It was said that he did not specify any amount but asked Dohrman to suggest this to Nagel. Dohrman claimed he refused the request.

That was all contained in the FBI interview of April 30th to which both Nagel and Dohrman signed their names.

Although Stephan, and even Salowich, were grasping at the "Nagel connection" it really was of no interest to Judge Tuttle. He felt, logically enough, that insofar as Stephan was concerned, it was an unimportant incident. A large portion of the crime had already been committed at that point and whether or not Nagel knew anything about Krúg was not a factor in Stephan's guilt. The only real issue was that if there was any truth in it, Nagel should be charged with a criminal act for concealing it.

The FBI had probably decided that Nagel would not be prosecuted even before their interview with him. A week earlier Erna Schwartz, the waitress, had been questioned at length. The thrust of the interview was in regard to whether or not she had observed Stephan and Nagel together on that night. The interview seemed to indicate that she had not, and there was every reason to believe that if Stephan joined Nagel at his table at all, it was for a very brief time period. She had not seen them engage in any conversation.

By the time Nagel's interview with the FBI was concluded the whole Nagel issue was put to rest by the Government. Nagel was not questioned again.

On May 3, 1943 Salowich had a diversion from the Stephan case, but one closely related to it. Theodore Donay's trial commenced on that date. The FBI had sought Krug's testimony in the same manner as they had in Stephan's case. A series of friendly visits were conducted. This time they found that Krug wanted to build a model airplane and they brought him the necessary supplies. Krug later displayed the plane to the agent. Another time Krug requested some American music. He had acquired a saxophone and had become a good enough player to be in the 35 piece camp orchestra. One of Krug's favorite pieces was "Home on the Range" and he had made a special arrangement so that it could be played by the orchestra. He became so good with the saxophone that he could transpose from one key to another on sight.

He requested news clippings dealing with the Detroit case, particularly those with his name and photo. The FBI furnished some and continued to reinforce the point that he was needed to "tell the truth."

So Krug, who had just turned 23, was back in town for a repeat performance. Although few allied prisoners managed to gain weight in German prison camps, Krug was noticeably heavier and had grown a mustache. His Canadian guards were highly amused by his latest book interest and could not resist telling about it. While being held in temporary quarters near Windsor he had acquired a copy of *See Here, Private Hargrove* which he was avidly reading. The book was a simple work of light humor about a draftee's experiences and Krug was said to be enjoying it immensely. When commenting on it he said that he guessed all soldiers and all armies were the same. No one would have been laughing, however, if they had known what was on Krug's mind. He was busily plotting a new escape. The change in appearance had its reasons and the book was undoubtedly being read to learn more about American slang.

Krug's testimony was much the same as that at the trial of Stephan. Krug testified that Donay knew who he was, a fact that Donay had denied. When it was his turn to cross-examine, Salowich got right to the point with Krug;

> Salowich: You refused to testify yesterday [as to] just why you are here.
> Krug: I don't want to tell it but believe me I don't want to make it worse for the defendant. The reason is a military secret.
> Salowich: Don't you know you are giving testimony for the U.S. Government.
> Krug: I am not a witness for the U.S. Government, I am a witness for myself.
> Salowich: I don't care whether you think it or not, you are a Government witness no matter what you think.

At that point, Judge Picard, the presiding Judge, intervened saying that he only wanted the truth and did not care who was a witness for who. Salowich had no better a relationship with Picard than he had with Tuttle. He was cognizant of the Judge's attitude since he, Picard, would occasionally insert comments about his two boys in the service. Following Picard's comments, Krug refused to answer questions and was removed.

Later that day FBI agents visited Krug and told him how disappointed they were with him. They told him that they had taken him at his word as a German officer and he had solemnly promised to testify. Krug jumped to his feet and said, "go tell the Judge I will be back tomorrow and take the stand. For what I did today I am sorry. Tomorrow I will erase the memory of today."

Krug went back to court the next day but insisted on reading a statement before testifying. He said, "what happened yesterday was just the last stone I needed in my picture about the situation in this case. It is entirely up to me to take the witness stand or to refuse it. I am therefore no ordinary witness, neither the Government's nor anybody else's witness. I am responsible to my superiors for what happened around my flight. I take the stand today. Therefore there must be some reason. It is certainly not the reason to make things worse for the defendant. That does not influence the truth a bit. That's the basis for today." Professor Bihl was probably not present at Donay's trial or he would have given Krug a little help with the statement.

Donay had tried to frantically motion, gesture, grimace, and otherwise signal to Krug, so at the start of the second day of Krug's testimony a wall of FBI agents stood between the two. That would seem to have been as good a message as any Donay could have sent. But Krug's statement did little to clarify anything and his appearance at Donay's trial, while Stephan was under a death sentence added to the mystery at the time, of why he was testifying.

Deitrich Rintelin testified at the trial, also, and disclosed the 30 hour lapse, between his call and the arrest at the restaurant. Not long after the trial, Rintelin volunteered for the armed forces.

Donay testified on his own behalf and even claimed to have many Jewish friends. The prosecution refuted this with the many anti-Semetic pieces of evidence, such as the poem quoted earlier. Also, among his list of claims was one that he feared the FBI agents, who had threatened to beat him and kill him.

Donay was, of course, found guilty by a jury that deliberated a total of 54 minutes. Judge Picard fined him $1,000 and sentenced him to 6 1/2 years in prison which was in addition to the year he had served while awaiting trial. Judge Picard was upset because he felt that the sentence, the maximum he could give, was far too lenient for the crime. Donay was sent back to Milan Penitentiary where he had been held for the previous year. His cell was close to Stephan's and the pair had, over the past year, engaged in occasional name calling. In one of these arguments their breakfasts had been brought to their cells and the food was cold. Stephan said it was alright, "just like down in Detroit," and Donay called out that Stephan would agree to any damn thing. Stephan told Donay that if it were not for him he would still be selling beer.

On May 7th Salowich was done with Donay and returned to Stephan.

Concurrently with Donay's trial, but not related to it, Lehr, Stephan's prosecutor, made his opinion officially known to his superiors. He wrote a letter to the Department of Justice in Washington in which he recommended a commutation of the death sentence. The letter, an amplification of the view he expressed to the jury, remained a secret until early July.

The outstanding business before the court for Stephan in early May was the appeal for a new trial. On May 7th Judge Tuttle denied the appeal and Salowich countered by entering a supplement to the motion for a new trial. He cited the 30 hour lapse between Dietrich Rintelin's call to the FBI and the arrest. Salowich had discovered that fact at Donay's trial and he contended that it constituted entrapment. The term entrapment simply means that if the authorities had not acted in a certain way, there would have been no crime. It is at least true that the most serious part of the whole affair, putting Krug on the bus, occurred long after the FBI was called. However, Stephan was already well into his crime by the time Rintelin called, and the claim of entrapment had little basis.

On May 13th Lehr, Babcock, and Salowich, along with Stephan, were back in court setting forth their respective arguments for and against a new trial. On May 22nd Tuttle again denied the petition and also delivered an opinion in which he reviewed the history of the case, including both appeals to higher courts. He also laid to rest one other issue dealing with the status of Stephan's citizenship. One contention had been that since Stephan had obtained his citizenship falsely, he was not really a citizen. That point led directly to the next one that claimed that since he was not a citizen he could not be tried for treason. It was essentially a case of one crime voiding another one and Tuttle would not hear of it. Citizenship obtained under false pretenses, said Tuttle, was voidable, but not void.

Later in May Detroit was concerned with the death of one of its more prominent citizens and Stephan was relegated to the back pages if he appeared at all. On May 26th Edsel Ford, the

49 year old only son of Henry Ford, died. His funeral and then his will were of prime interest.

On May 28th Salowich appealed the order denying a new trial. However, on June 1st the stay of execution, previously ordered by the Supreme Court, was, in legal language, vacated. Accordingly, Stephan was ordered to appear before Judge Tuttle on June 17th for the purpose of being sentenced once again. Everyone knew that this was the final countdown. Stephan had been in and out of Tuttle's courtroom many times, having been transported there time and again from Milan where he was still being held. He was, by then, little able to muster any composure in the courtroom. He would frequently weep openly. Salowich would kick him under the table, admonishing him to get himself under control.

At the resentencing Judge Tuttle gave another speech reminiscent of the one he had given earlier, back on August 6th, 1942, at the original sentencing. He said;

" . . . During that same ten months [since the original sentencing] millions of men and women have been working in our factories making the munitions of war costing billions of dollars for the very purpose of killing the enemies of this country. The people of this country believe it is necessary to do that dreadful thing. We are fighting for the accomplishment of that very thing and are buying bonds to accomplish it. Those German boys in the ranks of the enemy are not tainted by the disloyalty to the U.S. because they owe no loyalty to the U.S. Our millions of soldiers and billions of munitions are striving to take the lives of those enemy soldiers. Why? Because this is war and the most cruel war the world has ever known. We are fighting in self defense for our very lives as individuals and for our existence as a country. It must be that those who would hesitate to take the life of a traitor here on the home front who has tried to help Germany win this war are basing their conclusion on some false premise."

When his statement was concluded, Judge Tuttle set the execution date for July 2, 1943. Salowich felt that, as before, Tuttle looked more at him than at Stephan when he delivered the sentence. When it was over Salowich looked up at Judge

Tuttle and said, as he had said before, "he'll never hang, your Honor."

Judge Tuttle had not left much time between sentencing and execution. Furthermore, the appeal process had run its course and had proven futile. The only hope at this point was the direct intervention of President Roosevelt, who could then act, since there was no legal action pending.

Following the June 7th sentencing a number of groups and individuals became more active in trying to save Max Stephan. They all had one thing in common; a low regard for Stephan as a person, but a feeling that the penalty was far too harsh. The American Civil Liberties Union (ACLU) had obtained the signatures of 67 prominent citizens on a petition for clemency. The primary spokesman for the Detroit ACLU was Walter Nelson, the organization's local attorney, and the Reverend Henry Hitt Crane, Pastor of the Central Methodist Church. Nelson pressed the claim that even in England during the blitz, a person who did what Stephan had done, would have gotten about a two year jail sentence. He went on to say that we seemed to show a hysteria and blood thirstiness all out of proportion to what has happened to us.

Later in June, events in Detroit bordered on a national disaster and threatened to obliterate Stephan from anyone's mind. At that time the bloody 1943 race riots occurred. Trouble had been brewing for some time. There had been strikes at the war plants in which the main issue was simply that whites did not want to work with blacks. Vital production of tanks, guns, and other war material was halted over such grievances. At one of those strikes a passing sailor risked his neck by standing up to the crowd and imploring them to go back to work. It did no good but at least the crowd did not attack him.

The trouble started around Belle Isle and before it was over thousands of troops were called in. On June 23rd the death toll was 23 and would go much higher. Some say that the true death toll was never known and that it was really in the hundreds. It seemed as though more troops were being called in each day.

On June 23rd Salowich was unsuccessful in an attempt to see President Roosevelt about the case.

The President's file, even without a visit from Salowich, was growing, day by day. One thing was clear in the correspondence. People whose opinions were generally listened to were strongly advocating clemency. Appeals Court Judge Learned Hand was one such person. The negotiating committee of the United Rubber Workers of Detroit, however, urged that the sentence be carried out quickly (Appendix B1). On June 21st, Frederick Brown Harris, Chaplain of the Senate and Minister of the Foundry Methodist Church in Washington, wrote a letter to Attorney General Biddle. He sent a copy to Marvin McIntyre, Secretary to the President, asking him to please pass the letter on to the President. The letter pleaded for Stephan's life and quoted a conversation he had with Justice Murphy at the home of a mutual friend. It was claimed that Murphy had already "made a strong representation to the President" in favor of clemency (Appendix B2).

On June 24th Stephan wrote to President Roosevelt himself, to plead for his own life. Salowich had no knowledge of the letter. (The letter is contained in Appendix A1.)

It was transmitted by James Bennett, Director of the Bureau of Prisons, to Stephen Early, Secretary to the President. In his letter of transmittal, dated June 26th, Bennett erroneously addressed the letter to "Stephan" Early. President Roosevelt received the letter on June 29th and sent it to Biddle asking him if there was any truth in it or if it had any direct bearing on the case. Roosevelt was referring primarily to the Nagel affair which Stephan again discussed at some length. In his reply, Biddle gave further credence to the pomposity for which he was noted. He totally dismissed the contents of the letter as being nothing more than a rehash (Appendix A2). His comments about Nagel were strange for a legal minded person. He said, "Nagel is a man of good reputation and I am advised that his appearance and bearing inspire confidence. It is fair to assume that if he had been a witness at the trial he would have denied the whole transaction and would have been believed by the jury." Biddle's reply was received back at the White House on July 1st, the day before the scheduled execution.

Concurrently, however, a letter had been written to the President that finally made an intelligent summary of the anti-execution argument. It was written by a man who actually worked for Biddle. He was Charles Fahy, the Solicitor General, and his letter was written on June 30th, 1943 (Appendix A3). He explained that he had worked on the case when it went before the Supreme Court and was familiar with it. In his letter he included Prosecutor Lehr, although by title, not by name, among those who felt that the sentence was too severe. One of his points, coincidentally, touched on an earlier one mentioned by Nelson, the ACLU lawyer. Fahy told the results of a conversation he had with a Mr. Foster of the British embassy. The conversation was a brief inquiry on Fahy's part into how such cases might have been handled in England. Mr. Foster, later Sir John Foster, KBE,QC, was at the time the legal advisor at the British Embassy and held the rank of First Secretary in the Diplomatic Service. Mr. Foster had indicated that in all probability an English Max Stephan would have been charged with some crime not as severe as treason. Nevertheless, Fahy still felt that the charge of treason was correct. His contention was that death was too severe a penalty for Stephan's version. His exact wording was that, "Stephan's treason did not come of a plan maturely initiated by him to injure the country." He also brought up the point of the six saboteurs who were executed earlier and he compared their crime with Stephan's. He pointed out that since the minimum sentence for treason is five years, then it follows that the statutes recognize treason of different "qualities." It was interesting that the eventual White House press release also used the word "qualities." Another word, such as "degree" or "severity" could have been more fitting. There was that similarity and others between Fahy's letter and the press release. Fahy closed his letter with the comment that there would be criticism but that he thought most of the nonvocal people felt as he did.

Certainly the decision on Max Stephan was not as crucial as many that Roosevelt had been making. Not only that, but with the legal channels so completely supporting the sentence and the trial, Roosevelt could not really expect a great deal of criticism if he simply let the sentence stand. He had nothing to lose if he did nothing. Certainly no judge could criticise him.

On the morning of July 1st, no decision had yet been made. Just after noon on that day, with the actual execution just 12 hours away, two Detroiters put in a phone call to the White House. Doing the talking was Probate Judge Patrick H. O'Brien and at his elbow was Walter Nelson, the ACLU lawyer. O'Brien put his call through the Marvin McIntyre, the President's secretary and there were indications that Roosevelt was either near at hand or listening in. Roosevelt, of course, had Fahy's letter fresh in his mind.

O'Brien set forth his argument for clemency. He repeated the comparison with English penalties, unknowingly reinforced by Fahy's letter. Then he put forth his two major points; first, he said, the German people had been told that Roosevelt was bloodthirsty. This was a chance to show the Germans that defeat would not be so bad, democracy was humane. Second, O'Brien simply tried to make the point that it was the custom in a democracy to temper a sentence with mercy.

In the previous few weeks Justice Murphy had, on a number of occasions discussed the case with the President and also pleaded for commutation. So, just after noon on July 1st, the President had three strong pleas for mercy before him; Fahy's, Murphy's, and O'Brien's. With the execution imminent, the Detroit News summarized the positions of both sides of the issue. In closing, they waxed poetic, saying, "the hangman, saying nothing, tested his hempen rope."

About mid-afternoon on July 1st, President Roosevelt made his decision to commute Stephan's death sentence to life imprisonment.

A press release was quickly drafted. In an apparent attempt to placate the pro-execution faction, it started by decategorically stating that Stephan was indeed guilty of treason and had been properly convicted. (The press release is in Appendix C.) The release then explained the reasons for clemency which were essentially a repeat of Fahy's points. Roosevelt closed with a plea to future presidents, stating his hope, real or imaginary, that none of them would reduce the life sentence. None did, but as it turned out, only one could have.

The actual time of the execution had been set for 1:30 A.M. on July 2nd. While a closely guarded secret, it had somehow been "leaked" to Stephan. By mid-afternoon on July 1st he could then see the approach of death, scarcely ten hours away. The special permits to view the hanging had been issued, although one had no taker. Salowich had turned his down, saying he did not have the heart to go. For others it was a command performance. There were three doctors, six newsmen (Only three had been permitted to see Chebatoris hang), five official witnesses, marshals, the Chaplain, and of course, the hangman, for a total of twenty-two. In keeping with tradition, the hangman's name was not revealed. He was listed as Mr. Ellis, a pseudonym, so we are denied knowing if Hanna was given the job.

On July 1st a contractor was standing by to quickly assemble the scaffold as soon as darkness fell. A workman was ready to dig a two foot hole under the trap door. Others were ready to put a huge tarpaulin around the scaffold so that none but the chosen could see. All would undo their work before daylight on July 2nd. Steven Bush, a funeral director with a contract covering Federal prisoners was prepared to claim the body. He would be paid $25 to bury Stephan. Mrs. Stephan was said to be ill and had not been brought for a final meeting with her husband.

When Roosevelt made his decision, word was immediately sent to James Bennett, the Director of Federal Prisons. He, in turn, called Warden Shuttlesworth at Milan at 4:55 PM when the execution was scarcely eight hours from taking place. Shuttlesworth could do nothing until word was received by telegram. Regardless, he felt that Salowich should break the news to his client.

Earlier that day Stephan had once again broken down in his cell. He had been having nightmares about a scaffold and had been quoted as saying, "I've died a thousand deaths on it." Early in the afternoon of July 1st, knowing nothing of the events in Detroit and Washington, despondent, and resigned to his fate, Stephan wanted to talk to someone. He summoned Salowich from Detroit by telegram. Salowich received the wire, got in his car, and drove to Milan. He had been too depressed to turn on his car radio. If he had he would have heard the news before he arrived. At 5:25 P.M., thirty minutes after Shuttlesworth had received the word, Salowich entered the prison.

A reporter was also there and Salowich said to him, "you know, I never thought Maxie would hang but I'm getting jittery about that expected miracle."

A guard standing nearby told Salowich that the miracle had happened, "your client isn't going to hang."

Salowich said, "you wouldn't kid me, would you?"

Salowich gave a shout and said, "lead me to him."

Warden Shuttlesworth led the way to Stephan's cell. When they got there Salowich said, "Max, you're saved."

Stephan looked at Shuttlesworth for confirmation. Shuttlesworth said, "That's right, I just got it from Washington." Stephan fell to his knees, kissing the hands of Salowich and Shuttlesworth. A photographer took a picture of him at that instant and opponents of clemency later referred to Stephan "grovelling" on the floor.

Stephan then asked Shuttlesworth, "please, may I sleep with my door open tonight and without these awful lights," referring to the lights that were kept on him for surveillance.

Shuttlesworth said, "sure you can Max, and tomorrow you can get up and scrub out your cell just like the other prisoners do."

It was eight hours from the scheduled hanging.

His supper tray, the food untouched, was nearby and Stephan commented on it and talked a little, "I'm not hungry, not even now, I feel sick, I suppose it is the reaction. In the last year I have died a thousand times but I never really gave up until this afternoon. That's why I sent that wire to you Mr. Salowich, asking you to come here, I had to talk to someone. I know you promised me I'd never hang, Mr. Salowich, but it was close, too close." He then asked Salowich to send a wire to Agnes in Texas.

The agony was over. Salowich had successfully fought his delaying action, buying time while the proclemency forces built their case. That was his contribution. He never achieved his personal aim, that of getting a definition of treason from the Supreme Court. More than anything, he deserves credit for taking the case and seriously pursuing it, in the face of shattering abuse. Salowich was a strong man, both physically and mentally and Stephan was lucky to have had him for a lawyer.

Roosevelt deserves full credit for a just and humane decision, and one that he did not even have to make. Predictably, he received both praise and criticism when it was over.

Judge Tuttle would not comment. He told reporters, "you might as well save your shoe leather, boys, I have nothing to say."

The FBI was then in the process of deciding what to do with the two truckloads of material that they had removed from Donay's store. Most of it was at the Riverside Storage Company and some disposition would have to be made of it.

Chapter 11

The Case is Closed

The reaction to clemency was predictably mixed. Adolph Rosvek of Appoline Street in Detroit was pleased. He won $2,000 in a bet. Not only that, but the loser, who wished to remain anonymous, had given him 20 to 1 odds. Mrs. Ribble of Metamora, one of the members of the jury, was outraged. The rest of the jury was less vocal.

Salowich was greeted by old friends who had not spoken to him for a long time. He was no longer the "traitor's lawyer." Now he was a hero and they wanted to slap him on the back and renew old friendships. Some even asked if he could possibly get a piece of wood from the scaffold for a souvenir. "Sadistic bastards," he called them.

Roosevelt, of course, received his share of correspondence from all over the country, from the known and the unknown. A letter of criticism came from a Mr. V.J. Obenauer, the Secretary of the Associated Dailies of Florida, an organization of Florida newspapermen. A Mrs. Kenneth Long of Rochester, Michigan compared Roosevelt to Hitler and closed with, "such action makes patriotic people who love their country ashamed to call Franklin Roosevelt an American."

On the other hand, Supreme Court Justice Jackson sent a handwritten note that read, "I am glad and think it both wise and just that you have commuted the death sentence of Max Stephan. In calmer times, whatever the technical merits of the case, the court's sentence will seem savage in proportion to the offense. Thank God war does not distort your own sense of the fitness of things."

Charles Fahy, earlier supporter of clemency, sent the President some newspaper clippings supporting the decision. Another writer sent an editorial that criticized the decision. Probate Judge Patrick O'Brien of Detroit wrote to Marvin McIntye thanking him for his help and going on to say that the decision had been well received in the Detroit area. (Appendix D. contains some of the pro and con correspondence sent to the President.)

Walter Nelson, the ACLU lawyer said that the decision was gratifying. Meanwhile, a veterans' group was preparing to protest, but of course, the decision was final.

In the Supreme Court, new treason cases were appearing on the docket.[11] Immediately after Stephan's case, the Supreme court was presented with the first of several treason cases it would hear, out of the dozen treason cases to come out of World War II. Two of the cases were directly linked to the six saboteurs who were executed the day after Stephan's sentencing. The first case was the United States vs. Cramer. Cramer was a friend of one of the saboteurs, a certain Werner Thiel. Thiel had left the U.S. and returned as a saboteur. He then contacted Cramer, a friend from his earlier U.S. residency period. Cramer had little doubt what Thiel was doing, and met with him in a restaurant where FBI agents witnessed them in serious discussion. Cramer helped Thiel, held money for him, contacted his girl friend for him, and met with another saboteur, Kerling, who was Thiel's boss. The Supreme Court held that the conversation witnessed by the FBI was not treasonable because it took "imagination" to say that anything treasonous was being discussed. They defined a need for both intent and act, for treason to occur. Professor Hurst, in *The Law of Treason in the United States* gives the following example: If someone leads a strike in a war plant and the intent is money, the crime is not treason. If the intent is to harm the war effort, the crime is treason. Cramer became a landmark case but many felt that the Court had simply invented an issue and, in the process, created "bad law." Incidently, the Court was split, five to four, in that decision, which means that we probably could have gotten about as good a legal decision if we had simply asked the first person in the phone book.

Cramer was in late 1943, just after Stephan. Following Cramer was Haupt.[11] Haupt was the father of one of the saboteurs. He had helped his son buy a car, get a job, and generally get himself situated. This time the Court decided that the acts were so blatantly treasonous that the intent issue was not of concern. The whole issue was really becoming cloudier, rather than more clear. The Haupt case did help clarify the issue of two witnesses, however. Both the salesman and the sales manager at a car dealership, had witnessed parts of the auto purchase. However, neither had witnessed the entire transaction. The Court said that they still qualified as two witnesses to the same overt act. Another clarification in Haupt resulted from the unique relationship; father and son. Was the father helping the son only because he was his son or was it treason, or was it a little bit of both? The Court majority believed that it was both, but as long as some treason was involved, then the crime was treason. In other words, treason is the small bacteria that taints the whole bowl of potato salad. So Haupt served to clarify Cramer and the legal eagles were having a field day.

The Court had not really clarified anything, but it was the stuff that Salowich must have dreamed of when he took the case. Unfortuately, Stephan was just too clear-cut and Salowich must have been frustrated to find himself on the sidelines, watching others debate the issues that he had tried to raise.

The Solicitor General, Fahy, who was involved in Stephan's case, and Cramer's, later became a Circuit Court Judge and ruled on at least one treason case there.

Once Stephan's sentence was commuted, prison authorities were only concerned with settling Stephan into the routine of prison life. It was necessary that he simply become a regular prisoner, in his case, a lifer. Therefore, on July 8th, seven days after commutation, and a year after his arrival at Milan, Stephan was transferred to the huge Federal Prison in Atlanta, Georgia. Such dignitaries as Al Capone have been incarcerated there. Salowich never had any further contact with him and the possibility of a reduced sentence never came up.

The news of Max Stephan's reprieve was quickly known in the POW camps at Bowmanville and at Gravenhurst where Krug was held. When he learned of it he felt relieved but continued to really be more concerned for the other participants who seemed to be innocent victims, such as the Bertelmann family. He still felt that Stephan was more a victim of his own stupidity than anything else.

A month after the sentence was commuted, to the very day, Krug escaped again in a plan that, as it was told in the German book, *Escape Kings of Canada*,[10] was even more intricate than the earlier escape. The details are suspicious on several counts.

Gravenhurst was an Army camp, with the prison inside it. The guards were, in fact regular army soldiers. After one escape involving six prisoners, the guards beat the escapees severely when they caught them just outside the fence. It was part of the risk, though, and Waller, who had made the dummies in Krug's earlier escape, received two broken ribs. The beatings were simply an open manifestation of the fact that the Canadians' patience was being worn extremely thin.

Krug's escape took place on August 2nd, 1943 and since the preparation had taken two months, he must have started planning it in early June, a month before Stephan's last scheduled execution date. It probably never occurred to him if he escaped during the appeal process, it could bring negative publicity to Stephan. Anyway, twice a week in the warm months, the prisoners were allowed to go swimming in nearby Lake Muskoka. The beach where they did this was inside the Army camp.

Krug developed a plan whereby no alarm would be raised, similar in nature to the plan with the dummies. First, he developed a habit of wearing a red swimming cap for which he became known among the guards. Then he somehow made or acquired two wardrobes. They consisted of a civilian suit and a Canadian Captain's uniform. Actually Krug would attempt to resemble the camp interpreter, a Captain Surow who carried a walking stick with a silver head. Krug would also carry a walking stick but the head of his would be made from a shaving cream bottle cap.

On the appointed day, 72 prisoners showed up to go swimming, an unusually large number. Krug's bathing suit looked a little strange because under it he also wore two pair of pants, rolled up. The uniform pants were over the civilian ones. He situated himself near the middle of the column and the prisoners around him had other articles of clothing rolled up in their towels and jackets.

Guards were at the front and rear of the column as it moved out. Walter Manhart was at the end and he carried a bag of candy. As the column went around a bend, the rear guards were out of sight of the front guards. At that moment Manhart dropped the bag, bursting it, and spilling the candy. He and two other prisoners stopped to pick up the candy and the guards had to pause for a minute with them. The prisoners could not, of course, be left behind. In the middle of the column Krug made his metamorphosis. Other prisoners tore off his coat and helped with his shirt, uniform, coat, and hat. Another handed him his walking stick while he handed another his red swimming cap.

In an instant he disappeared into some scrub. He walked toward the officers' club and somehow left the camp, quickly discarding the uniform. Then he took a ferry which regularly crossed a narrow neck of the lake.

Meanwhile Manhart had picked up the candy and the column of prisoners was at the beach. Soldiers were already posted there to stand guard. As the swimmers were diving and splashing, someone shouted that Krug had drowned. Manhart ran up to a guard with the red cap, saying it was all he had been able to grab. Everyone started diving for Krug. Later the Canadians began diving operations for the body. Failing to find him, they even used dynamite. Finally, on the third day, word was sent to Ottawa that prisoner 52021, Peter Krug, had drowned. Almost simultaneously he entered the railway station in North Bay, Ontario, a hundred miles north of Gravenhurst. If we are to believe the story, the Military Police officer in the station was one of the Canadians who had received Krug at the border when the FBI returned him after the Texas episode. The officer supposedly recognized Krug immediately and turned him over to the Mounted Police.

As mentioned, the story is suspicious on several counts. For example if he was reported drowned, his parents would have been notified. With a brother on the Russian front, it is hard to understand how he could justify causing them so much anguish.

The Canadian version is somewhat simpler. They say that Krug escaped on August 2, 1943, wearing bathing trunks. On the morning of August 5th he was recaptured while walking toward the North Bay railway station. He was wearing Army trousers and a windbreaker. He was asked where he was going and replied, "Oh, nowhere in particular, why do you ask?" The authorities noted that when captured he was eating a candy bar.

Small events connected with the Stephan case continued to crop up. On November 8, 1943, the last letter came in to President Roosevelt in regard to the case. It was from Judge Tuttle and he urged that Stephan's citizenship not be revoked. He explained that such action could result in Stephan being returned to Germany after the war and not serving his full sentence.

A little over a year later, on December 3, 1944, Judge Tuttle died at Henry Ford Hospital in Detroit. He was 76 years old. Following funeral services in Detroit his body was returned to Leslie, Michigan for burial. Papers throughout the country, including the New York Times, carried his obituary. Most made some reference to the Stephan case, even mentioning Krug. At least one noted that Stephan was still in prison.

Back in the POW camps the old "Battle of Britain" prisoners were gradually receiving promotions.[10] Steinhilper, one of the prisoners who used the "dummy" and "workman" trick before Krug, was now *Hauptmann* (Captain) Steinhilper. In 1945 he perpetrated one of the more bizarre escape attempts of the whole group.[10] After seeing several prisoners exchanged, including Hasso von Wedel, he decided he would try to feign insanity and inspire the Canadians to exchange him. He was injured in a hockey game and decided to let the resulting blow to the head be the start of his plan. For a short time he performed various irrational acts. He went berserk, slashed himself with broken glass, and once jumped out of a second story window. Finally the Canadians committed him to an insane asylum. Once there, he was fed and injected with drugs and lived with what may have been the worst of the patients. As part of the deception he ate little food and lost about 40 pounds. The culmination of the story was that by the time the Canadians were convinced of his insanity, the war was nearly over and the exchanges were discontinued. He then had to fake a recovery and was eventually returned to a POW camp. It was an experience that could have caused permanent brain damage, drug addiction, or could have had lasting physical effects. In corresponding with Steinhilper, 30 years later, he certainly seemed fit and able. His English was good and I could only suspect that he was a prosperous business man. He was open and honest, and not the least bit given to bragging about his exploits.

By May of 1945, Hitler was dead and Germany had collapsed. On V-E day, May 8, Peter Krug may have witnessed the townspeople of Gravenhurst, Ontario who marched, cheering and shouting, past the camp.[7] At Bowmanville, General von Ravenstein spoke to the assembled prisoners. He told them how he had seen defeat in 1918, also, and understood how they felt. He went on to tell them that it was better that Germany lost. He said that he believed that if Germany had won, they would have lost their souls, their honor.[7] It was a speech that came right from the mists of Germanic antiquity. And it was true. These were men who had vehemently demanded "proper" treatment from their captors. They were soldiers and believed that they had fought the good fight, honestly and fairly. But that was the lie of Naziism and von Ravenstein knew it. One cannot fight honorably for a dishonorable cause, and their illusions of honor were nothing more than a golden temple built on quicksand. In Europe the death camps, where six million Jews had been murdered, were being photographed and documented. It was more than ugly.

For the prisoners, freedom was still more than a year away, but they were still the lucky ones. For hundreds of thousands of their comrades, it had been death in an unmarked grave in Russia.

In the U.S., also, the era of the prisoners was coming to a close. In Missouri, *Afrika Korps* prisoners had built a 200 acre scale model of the Mississippi River system that served well in flood control analysis for many years. In the rural counties of Michigan they had worked on the farms and enjoyed the same sort of freedom that their Canadian counterparts had enjoyed. In Utah in July of 1945, eight of them died at the hands of a berserk guard who opened fire on a camp with his machine gun.

It is believed that at the end of the war, about 200 German and Italian escapees were unaccounted for, but still, only von Werra had succeeded in returning to Europe.

In August of 1945, atomic bombs were dropped on Hiroshima and Nagasaki. It would provide philosophers with thesis material, probably forever, but few of them were in the army at the time, preparing for the invasion of mainland Japan. The Japanese, with visions of their cities disappearing, one at a time, in blinding flashes, realized the futility of continuing the war. On the 14th of August they surrendered and World War II was history.

Frank Murphy, friend of William Nagel and the Supreme Court Justice who had been instrumental in saving Stephan's life, became involved in more of the same.[8] U.S. authorities in Japan, under the direction of General MacArthur, were eager to bring to justice the Japanese military leaders who had, with such facile, committed horrible atrocities against their enemies in such acts as the Bataan Death March. General Homma, the Japanese General who was in charge of the Philippine campaign, and incidently, MacArthur's direct opponent in that battle, was sentenced to death. The Supreme Court reviewed the matter and Murphy, along with Justice Wiley Rutledge, vehemently opposed the death penalty for Homma, particularly because it was pressed by MacArthur, the man that Homma had defeated. Murphy was on the losing side of that issue.

Stephan remained at Atlanta until August 7, 1951. By that time his adopted country had finished one war and had become involved in another. But Max Stephan was a sick man and was then transferred to the Medical Facility for Federal Prisoners at Springfield, Missouri. Mrs. Stephan was on his approved list of visitors and did, on occasion visit him. The circumstances of her visits are not known, nor is it known what happened to her when the war was over. That information is considered to be confidential by both the prison authorities and the Immigration Department. It is believed, by some, that she had not been deported after the war, and may have been allowed to stay because of Max.

On January 13, 1952, at the age of 59, Max Stephan died at the Springfield Medical Center. In medical terms the cause of death was uremia due to adenocarcinoma of the sigmoid colon. In layman's language it was cancer of the large bowel. He had been long forgotten by all but a few and no public mention was made of his passing. Even though Nicholas Salowich passed through Atlanta several times, he never visited Stephan. He had been his lawyer, not his friend.

Two years later William Nagel died at the age of 81.

Peter Krug had been returned to Germany in November, 1946. His first job was as laborer-apprentice in a steel mill. That was followed by other jobs and in 1952 he went into business for himself as a manufacturer's representative. Soon after starting the business he moved to Letmathe, a small town near Dortmund, where he settled permanently. In 1955 he married and later a son and a daughter were born. Through others one can learn that he has become a successful businessman. The wish to pilot an airplane, described to the newspaper reporters by Max Stephan, never went away. In the early fifties, as a hobby, he took up glider flying and later airplanes. The hobby was continued and later he became the proud possessor of a commercial pilot's license.

In 1953 he saw the name of Chemnitz, the city where his family settled in 1924, disappear from the maps. The city was in Communist East Germany, and in typical communist fashion its name was changed to Karl Marx Stadt (Karl Marx City).

In 1956 some of Krug's old friends may have returned to the U.S. on an official basis. In that year a revitalized *Luftwafe* began training exercises at Luke Air Force Base in Arizona. The German Commander, Lieutenant Colonel (*Oberstleutnant*) Horst Wilhelms, related in a letter some "things" that he knew "for sure". One was that Krug had successfully made it back to Germany and another was that he had then been shot down and killed. Of course, Wilhelms had confused Krug with von Werra, a common error.

That was also about the time when the stories of the "Escape Kings" were published in serial form in *Stern*. Krug's 1942 escape was described in one of the installments (*Ein Leutnant Reist Nach Mexiko*; A Lieutenant Travels Toward Mexico). The story was accompanied by a map of Germany and the U.S., to the same scale, thus emphasizing the magnitude of the 5,000 kilometer trip, which was shown on the U.S. map. A picture of a Greyhound bus was included. There were also photos of the former Lieutenant as he appeared in *Luftwaffe* dress uniform and with his "white sidewall" haircut and borrowed glasses in the identification picture. The article left out all reference to his appearance at the trial, his testimony, and, of course, his reasons for testifying.

One person in Germany read Krug's story with particular interest and could well remember that day in 1942, on Philip Street in Detroit, when he knocked on her door. After the war Mrs. Bertelmann divorced her husband, for not visiting her while she was in the detention camp,[9] and returned to Germany. By 1956 she had remarried. Upon seeing the article in *Stern* she contacted Peter Krug and then, with her new husband, visited him in Letmathe. Photos of the reunion were carried in *Stern*. She and Krug kept in touch after that and continued even after the former Mrs. Bertelmann had again left Germany. Actually, she returned to the U.S., and eventually lived in a trailer park in San Diego. She refused to talk about the case and apparently reprimanded Krug for even giving out her address. She must have returned illegally with her new husband.

The 1956 stories, serialized in *Stern*, were put in book form and titled *Escape Kings of Canada (Ausbrecher Konige von Canada)*. It was done partly in response to the desire of children and families of the POWs, who wanted to know more about the experiences in Canada. The book was fictionalized by adding conversations that never could have occurred and at least one escapee, Ulrich Steinhilper, was not entirely happy with it. He didn't particularly care for the title and felt that the dangerous and difficult aspects of the escapes had been trivialized.

In modern Detroit much has changed. The trolleys are gone and the skyline is different. But one can cross over to Windsor and go out along Riverside Drive, past Dieppe Street, and look across at Belle Isle. It looks like a good place to cross and in spite of Judge Tuttle's suspicions, that was where Krug stole or took the rowboat and paddled over. The distance is shorter than anywhere else and from that viewpoint you can't really tell that you are looking at an island. In Detroit the half mile long Belle Isle Bridge still meets the mainland near the spot where Stephan once had his restaurant. The restaurant is gone, though, and in its place there is just an empty paved lot next to a hamburger joint. From the end of the Belle Isle Bridge to Mrs. Bertelmann's house, by the most direct route, is a five mile trip. The route goes by the Whittier hotel where John Bugas once lived. At the end of the five mile trip, however, where the Bertelmann's flat once stood, there is now an empty lot. Strangely, it is the only vacant lot in the entire block and looks like a missing tooth.

Nicholas Salowich moved his law office from Detroit to Southfield where he and one of his sons, Nicholas Jr., practiced from the same building. Nicholas Jr. explained that his father's clients had generally become his father's personal friends, also. This was true of Donay, for whom Salowich Sr. had performed legal services for some time prior to the Stephan case. It is doubtful that Salowich ever received any money from Donay for his handling of the case. Even the prior legal work had generally been paid for in dusty German music boxes and the like, which Donay had on his shelves. Nicholas Jr. remembers visiting Donay's store, as a boy of 13, with his father. Donay sometimes gave him a bottle of imported loganberry flavoring which the young Salowich would take home and use to make flavored soda pop.

Donay served his full sentence of six and one half years in prison. After his release he went to California. One day in April of 1950 he bought 10 feet of chain, some soldering wire, and a pair of pliers. He wrote a suicide note and left it in his hotel room. The next day the police found a boat, rented in his name, floating near Catalina Island. It is safe to assume that he really did commit suicide. The part that is hard to understand is why he didn't do it in prison, years earlier. To serve seven and a half years, pay his debt to society, so to speak, and then commit suicide, is strange, to say the least. But Donay was a strange person. He must have found himself frozen in time, somewhere back in the thirties. In 1950 the world was vastly changed and his cause was lost and discredited. His manners and customs would have been laughable. Maybe he was just too inflexible to adapt. We really don't know. He chose a hard way to die, however. One would think it would have been easier to simply open a vein.

Nicholas Salowich died in 1976 at the age of 82. He worked until the end. He was going to see someone in downtown Detroit, around Fort and Griswold. He parked his car and, from all indications, peacefully slumped over his steering wheel.

Over the years, Max Stephan's treason story appeared, possibly twice, in Sunday Magazine sections of Detroit papers. Its last appearance was in February, 1976. That was an accurate and well-written account, except for one point—the author confused Krug and von Werra. Aside from those two stories and the mention of the case in Tuttle's obituary, it became a forgotten case.

If you drive up in Michigan's Thumb to the town of Harbor Beach, you can see the house where, in 1890, Frank Murphy was born. A Michigan historical marker has been placed in front of it, telling of his term as Michigan Governor and of his appointment to the Supreme Court.

Not far from there, 17 miles west of Port Huron, is the town of Emmett where Jerry Armstrong, the jury foreman lived. He died in the mid 60's but his substantial Michigan farmhouse is still there, wooden letters on the fence post spelling the name of Armstrong.

At Bowmanville, Ontario the old camp has been modernized and returned to its role as a boy's reformatory. The people in the area, those who were there during the war, still remember the "trouble in camp" and the fire trucks racing out there with hoses to help put down the riots. Some of the old POWs, "Bowmandorfers" included, came back and settled permanently in Canada. The Bowmanville "Alumni Association" meets occasionally to reminisce and stay in touch. Address lists are maintained and include "alumni" on both sides of the Atlantic. One of them, Doctor Vollmer, lives less than ten miles from his old POW camp and is certainly one of his town's more respected citizens. Peter Krug's address is still shown as the small town where he was visited by the former Mrs. Bertelmann. He has a fine home there, complete with a swimming pool. Although he has traveled extensively outside of Europe since the war, he has not returned to the U.S. or Canada for a visit.

As for his testimony at the trial, there is no real mystery. The FBI initiated the talks and apparently gave a convincing argument. Krug was only 22 at the time and really cannot be blamed for having been talked into it. He was, of course, completely lacking in any knowledge of the American legal system. He probably visualized a panel of judges hearing the testimony, as might happen in Germany, if you were lucky. Once he saw the system at Stephan's trial it is difficult to understand why he came back to Donay's trial. It could only be a case of overwhelming arrogance. One peripheral party to the case referred to him as an "arrogant jerk."

As mentioned earlier, the real mystery is why his superior officers did not see through the idea. It would seem that the real concern, from the prisoners standpoint, would be that after Krug gave testimony, and literally sold two people, Stephan and Donay, down the river for having helped him, no one in their right mind would ever help a German escapee again. That would seem to be the real issue for the prisoners. One could even dismiss the appearance at Stephan's trial as a mistake, but then we are still left searching for an excuse for the Donay appearance. Why someone in the officer ranks couldn't see it as a giant blunder is beyond comprehension.

Krug always believed that he did the right thing. He knew that Stephan was doomed, but felt that he had helped sort things out in respect to the others. Krug was quite proud of the fact that the FBI never found out about his other U.S. contacts.

The FBI records, which describe the case as "no ordinary crime," reflect a crisp, clean accounting of the process of gaining Krug's testimony.

In respect to the Government's case against Max Stephan, there were some serious weaknesses that were only touched on at the time. Stephan was charged with a long list of "overt acts," supposedly supporting the charge. Most of the acts had little to do with treason, as evidenced by Judge Tuttle's direction to throw out the one about the visit to the house of prostitution. The other overt acts dealing with various visits and trivial actions, also did not support a treason charge. In the whole case, sending Krug to the Field Hotel and putting him on the bus dealt with treason and there were not two witnesses to either of those acts.

Remaining is the question of why Max Stephan did what he did and the answer to that may be more easily explained than all the others. He described himself as a man who "takes the middle way." Salowich, in later years, when searching for a descriptive adjective, settled on "milksop." Certainly he was a man with few, if any, convictions about right and wrong. He had never taken his citizenship seriously, and much of his life had been spent in testing the limits of the law enforcement systems. Had he turned Krug in he could never have faced his lunatic peers. So with Stephan, the lack of moral conviction, along with a generous helping of peer pressure, all combined to overcome any fears or doubts he may have had. He simply took "the middle way." Donay was, indeed, more sinister.

Certainly Max Stephan did commit a very serious crime. By putting Krug on the bus, he caused a great deal of manpower to be diverted from other duties and sent in search of a fugitive. In wartime that is a very serious matter. Had Krug made good his escape we can surmise that Stephan would not have had his sentence commuted. Krug could have carried back valuable information and worse, could have again piloted a bomber. His reports of mistreatment would have caused greater hardships and death for Allied prisoners in Germany.

As far as the death sentence was concerned, the years make it seem even more harsh. Since the punishment for treason was on a scale that ran from five years to death, someone recognized various degrees of the crime. Therefore the death penalty, at the top of the scale, should have been reserved for those making a more direct form of war against the U.S. on a premeditated basis. The government prosecutor, Lehr, and his staff, never believed that Stephan deserved the death penalty. Undoubtedly, it was their objective to use the man as an example to certain citizens, but not to the extent that Tuttle chose. It was a time of stress, and Tuttle most certainly believed that he was contributing to the war effort, in his own way, by setting an example with Stephan.

In order to understand Judge Tuttle and more particularly his history of harsh sentences, one can spend a few hours in Leslie, Michigan. The town cemetery has few, if any, monuments higher than the "Tuttle" spire. It carries only the family name and around it, identified by identical stones, are the last resting places of the various family members. John J., the Judge's grandfather and the man who came from New York to homestead in the area, was born in 1812 and died in 1903, at the age of 91. His wife Emma was born in the same year as he, but died in 1887 at the age of 75. Judge Tuttle's father, Ogden Valorous, was born in 1842 and died in 1916 at the age of 74. His wife, Judge Tuttle's mother, died in 1903 at the age of 63. Ogden apparently had a sister who died at the age of 19, but the grave site does not contain any other testimonies to those tragic early deaths, so common in old cemeteries. About four miles northwest of Leslie, across the expressway, one can see the old Tuttle homestead. It is on Annis Road, just off Tuttle Road, and is an impressive example of the better Michigan farmhouses of its era. A short way down Annis Road from the house is a six foot stone monument with these words;

> "On this spot John J. and Emma A. Tuttle built their log cabin in 1837 and here Ogden V. Tuttle was born in 1842."

From the style of the printing it would seem that it was erected near the turn of the century, probably by Ogden Valorous. The location is odd since it is in a low, swampy part of the property. Of course, in 1837 the area must have been wooded and it may have been that a spring welled up near the site. Annis Road is really only used by local farmers and the inscription is on the side away from the road. Few people in Leslie have ever read the inscription since the price of reading it is a pair of muddy shoes.

The Tuttle name remains on the road but only some old timers in town remember the family and who they were.

But one thing is certain. Judge Tuttle's family is steeped in the American tradition of going west to seek opportunity, in breaking the land, in settling and putting down roots. Certainly a man with those traditions behind him, born to that land, whose grandfather built a log cabin with his bare hands, must have certainly had strong feelings about tradition and patriotism. His sense of reason may have been affected by it.

His death sentence in the Chebatoris case was clearly justified. Chebatoris committed the maximum crime, murder, and got the maximum penalty, death. In the case of Fisher and Zehnder in Frankenmuth, the penalty was totally out of proportion to the crimes. Tuttle simply leaned toward maximum penalties.

Fortunately for southeast Michigan, Fisher and Zehnder survived Judge Tuttle's near-disastrous fine. Today their restaurants are top tourist attractions and the town has become a sort of Disneyland. Unfortuately, when we drink our beer in either establishment we have to rest our elbows on modern formica bars instead of the solid oak that Judge Tuttle had destroyed.

To his credit, Jerry Armstrong, the jury foreman and insurance salesman from Emmett, Michigan, had the presence of mind to make the jury pause to reflect on their decision. For them there was only one conclusion. From that point, Max Stephan was in Judge Tuttle's hands and he acted in a manner consistent with his past sentences.

Nicholas Salowich deserves credit for a heroic effort. His desperate delaying action bought valuable time until Murphy, Fahy, and the others could make their point.

But there is one lone hero who must not be overlooked. President Franklin Delano Roosevelt, politician though he may have been, acted in a very unpolitical way and managed to restore sanity. And that was something that was badly needed in those days.

Appendix A.

Letters to President Roosevelt from:

1. Max Stephan
2. Attorney General Francis Biddle
3. Solicitor General Charles Fahy

P. M. Box 1000
Milan, Michigan
June 24, 1943

Hon. Franklin D. Roosevelt,
President of the United States,
White House,
Washington, D.C.

Dear Mr. President:

On Saturday, April 18, 1942, after showing this escaped prisoner of war a good time because it was his birthday, I had made my mind up to report this prisoner of war to Federal official B. Nagel of Seyburn Ave., Detroit, Mich. which I did. Nagel has been 35 years a Federal employee, has also been Postmaster of Detroit and was a Democrat all his life.

Mr. Nagel came this special evening to my restaurant and I reported to him the whole story. I had the greatest confidence in Mr. Nagel because he is a personal friend of Hon. Supreme Court Justice Frank Murphy and has a fine reputation all over Michigan. Whatever Mr. Nagel would have told me to do I would have done. Mr. Nagel told me then: "This is a prisoner of war; for him the war is over, it will be only a matter of a couple of days and he will be caught without me reporting him. His picture will be all over the United States." Mr. Nagel told me he would take him to Chicago in his car, if he had time, to let him have a few more days of freedom, and that I should bring him to the Bus instead of the train, the bus would be more liberal. After being so assured I brought him Sunday morning to the Bus Station. At 12 P.M. the same day the F.B.I. arrested me and I told them a full story of what happened.

In the County Jail my wife told me Mr. Nagel made an appointment over the phone to meet her on the street because he didn't want to be seen with her. He told my wife I had talked too much and I should not mention his name any more; he could help me more by leaving him out. Mr. Nagel also told my wife that he had been questioned by the F.B.I. and that he denied everything. I really kept Mr. Nagel out so long as possible but it still didn't do me any good.

I never was a member of any Nazi Society. I belonged to two American Political Clubs, the Joint and United Political Committee and the Steuben Society. Both Clubs did not take any campaign money from their candidates. All campaign expenses were

Hon. Franklin D. Roosevelt
President of the United States

#2

paid out of our own pockets. I never missed a vote, worked very hard before every election by sending out slates, going with a committee to different clubs to tell them to vote. I helped to arrange boat excursions to get some campaign money. I belonged to an investigating committee which talked to all our candidates before the election.

In the 15 years I have been in this country I have never sent a letter to Germany, not even to my relatives or communicated with anyone. My connections with Germany were entirely cut off. December the 17th, 1941 I bought $100 worth of War Bonds.

I really did not look for mercy. All I wanted is truth and justice, but the truth did not come out, so that I have to ask for mercy. Mr. Nagel is 70 years old now and a very strict Catholic and on his death bed he for sure would confess, so that I still have a chance to prove that I am not a traitor.

Very respectfully,

(signed) Max Stephan

Office of the Attorney General
Washington, D.C.

June 30, 1943

My dear Mr. President:

This is in response to your memorandum of today transmitting the letter of Max Stephan dated June 24, 1943, addressed to you and forwarded by the Director of the Bureau of Prisons. A copy of this letter had already been forwarded to me.

The instant letter is no more than an elaboration of a similar recital in a statement made by Stephan to an agent of the Federal Bureau of Investigation which is set forth on page 4 of my recent letter of advice in which it appears that about 11 o'clock on the night of April 18, 1942, one William J. Nagel went to Stephan's restaurant, and having been told the story of the escaped German war prisoner, advised Stephan that he (Nagel) would help the prisoner to go to Chicago.

As I pointed out in my previous letter, this incident, if it be true, took place after Krug (the prisoner) had left Stephan's restaurant and had put up for the night in a hotel and after Stephan had made inquiries as to train and bus transportation and had planned on sending the escaped prisoner to Chicago by bus on the following morning. It could not, therefore, have been the impelling cause of Stephan's determination to give aid and assistance to Krug.

2

The instant letter is virtually the same in all particulars as a letter addressed by Stephan on April 17, 1943, to Judge Tuttle at the instance of Mr. Justice Murphy of the Supreme Court of the United States. Copies of Stephan's letter and Justice Murphy's letter are herewith submitted. Following the prisoner's letter to Judge Tuttle a motion for new trial was filed embodying the same allegations with respect to the Nagel incident. The motion was denied by the District Judge on May 22, 1943, with an opinion, a copy of which is herewith submitted. The denial of the motion was affirmed by the United States Court of Appeals after hearing on June 22, 1943.

To the answer of the United States to the motion for new trial is appended an affidavit of William J. Nagel categorically and fully denying that he held any conversation with Stephan of the character alleged. Nagel admits that he visited Stephan's restaurant between 12 o'clock midnight on April 18 and 1 o'clock in the morning on April 19, and had a brief conversation with him but that nothing was said with respect to a German war prisoner or assistance to be given him. The Nagel affidavit is submitted herewith. Nagel's statement in that respect was in substance the same as that made by him to the Department's agents on November 22, 1942, when he was interviewed with reference to the statement made by Stephan at the time of his arrest.

3

In view of the foregoing it is my judgment that Stephan's recent letter to you contains nothing which has not already been carefully considered by the Courts with what seems to me to be the rightful conclusion that even if true, it was not newly discovered and that Stephan could have produced Nagel at his trial as a witness if the incident were in fact true.

Furthermore Nagel in his statement taken November 25, 1942, asserts that the alleged incident did not take place, and in his affidavit dated May 13, 1943, repudiates in detail all the statements contained in Stephan's letter to the Judge, his motion for new trial and his letter to you. Nagel is a man of good reputation, and I am advised that his appearance and bearing inspire confidence. It is fair to assume that if he had been a witness at the trial he would have denied the whole transaction and would have been believed by the jury.

In answer to your query I advise that I am not convinced of the truth of the statements contained in Stephan's letter to you and am firmly of the opinion that the letter has no material bearing on the case in its present status.

Respectfully,

(signed) Francis Biddle
Attorney General.

The President,
The White House.

Office of the Solicitor General
Washington, D.C.
June 30, 1943.

MEMORANDUM FOR THE PRESIDENT

Re: Application of Max Stephan for
commutation of death sentence.

The United States Attorney at Detroit who prosecuted Stephan for treason, consisting of aiding an escaped German prisoner of war, feels definitely that the sentence of death is too severe. He intimated this to the jury that convicted Stephan, though the sentence was not for the jury to fix. Honorable Wendell L. Berge, Assistant Attorney General in charge of the Criminal Division, is of the same opinion. I studied the case and filed the brief with the Supreme Court when Stephan sought review there of his conviction. The Supreme Court denied review, in accordance with the position taken by me. His trail was fair and free of reversible error. But I feel, too, that the sentence of death is too severe. The Chief Justice has advised me that there is a strong feeling within the Court, which he is inclined to share, that the sentence of death is too severe.

I have been advised informally (by Mr. Foster of the British Embassy) that in England one who did what Stephan did would probably not be tried for treason but under a statute not carrying the death sentence.

Although guilty of treason, our statute provides he shall suffer death or, at the discretion of the court, shall be imprisoned for not less than five years and fined not less than $10,000. Thus the statute contemplates, with respect to the sentence, treason of different qualities.

Stephan's treason did not come of a plan maturely initiated by him to injure the country or give aid and comfort to the enemy in the sense one ordinarily thinks of treason. The

-2-

escaped German prisoner arrived in Detroit and came to the doorway of a woman who had been sending food and clothing to German prisoners in Canada, in doing which she had been required to write her name and address on the packages. She communicated with Stephan, who assisted the escaped prisoner, knowing he desired to return to Germany to do his "duty again." The assistance consisted of taking him about Detroit, giving him a light traveling bag, assisting in procuring a prostitute, meals and a ticket to Chicago. The escaped prisoner was in Detroit about 24 hours, and Stephan helped him during that period in such ways as above, perhaps also in obtaining some $20.00 or so in money in addition to the ticket to Chicago.

It will be seen that, unlike the saboteurs, this was no well planned plot to do violence to the Nation. That he was properly convicted of treason, however, is true. That was the position I took in the Supreme Court. But I respectfully suggest that a lesser sentence, contemplated by the treason statute in some cases, is more appropriate for this conduct. The sentence of death should be reserved for those who have contributed in larger part or greater degree to the dark deeds of this war. Commutation to life imprisonment is desirable, I feel. You would be criticized. But I think most of the non-vocal people of the country feel as I do.

The Attorney General knows that I am stating my views to you. I told him I would like to do so and he assents to my doing so.

Respectfully,

(signed) Charles Fahy,
Solicitor General.

Appendix B.

Other Correspondence:

1. Wire from U.S. Rubber Workers Negotiating Team.
2. Letters from Frederick Brown Harris.

June 4, 1943

Respectfully referred to the Department of Justice for consideration and acknowledgment.

M. H. McIntyre
Secretary to the President

John Harmon, Pres. and others,
Local 101,
United Rubber Workers of America Plant Negotiating Committee,
Detroit, Michigan

Telegram to the President dated 6/4/43.

"Profoundly shocked at request for clemency for traitor Max Stephan while our boys are dying on the battlefront. Every agent of the enemy must pay the full price for his crime.

FREDERICK BROWN HARRIS
2800 THIRTY-SIXTY STREET, N.W.
WASHINGTON, D.C.

June 21, 1943

Hon. Marvin McIntyre,
The White House
Washington, D.C.

Dear Marvin:

You will of course have a chance to talk to the President about the Max Stephan case. The enclosed carbon of a letter I am sending to Attorney General Biddle expresses my feeling about this whole matter. I really am convinced that we will be doing our own cause a favor by letting this man live behind bars to witness the downfall of the devilish regime to which, even as a citizen of this country, he has been loyal. I will appreciate it if in talking this matter over with the President you would let him know that I have sent such a letter to the Attorney General, and, in a word, express my definite conviction that the United Nations' cause will be helped by letting this miserable creature live behind bars, instead of hanging.

With warm personal regards, I am,

Yours ever,

(signed) Frederick Brown Harris

FBH/bm

UNITED STATES SENATE
Office of the Chaplain

C-O-P-Y

Washington, D.C.
June 21, 1943.

The Honorable Francis J. Biddle,
The Attorney General,
Washington, D.C.

Dear Mr. Biddle:

Entirely on my own initiative and not as a part of any organized propaganda, I hope it will not be violating any propriety if I may express to you my personal feeling with regard to the present scheduled execution of Max Stephan.

You know, without my telling you, how I feel about Hitler and his works. I had the opportunity of saying to you personally at the Capitol a few days ago that there was the sound of a great amen in my heart to your classic message to Quisling. I was entirely in favor of the execution of the saboteurs, trained in Germany and landed on our shores with all the parapharnalia of destruction in their hands. But I have the deep conviction that it would be a great mistake to go ahead with the hanging of Stephan. Such an outcome of his offense would sever too much of what happened to Nurse Cavell in Belgium for harboring and aiding in escape British prisoners. That act on the part of German authorities has rightly become a byword and a hissing. I know that this is not analagous, yet somehow it just doesn't seem to be the American attitude to take a man's life because he harbored a couple of German agents, or prisoners, and sent them on their way by his connivance.

In talking to your predecessor, Associate Justice of the Supreme Court Murphy, yesterday at a home where we were both guests I find that he has already made a strong representation to the President with regard to his feeling about this matter. He is very much against the execution and in favor of commutation to a number of years that will insure that this man, who is an acknowledged rotter and a menace to society, will at least for a good many years be behind bars after his idol Hitler has been utterly defeated. I really believe that the intervention of the President before the date of execution, making the sentence Life Imprisonment instead of hanging, in this particular case, will react throughout the world to the benefit of the Allied cause. It will be recognized as a vivid illustration of the difference between the ways of democracy and the ways of the totalitarian state without pity or conscience. I send you this hoping that you will also take this attitude and will throw the weight of your great office and influence in favor of commutation.

With warm personal regards, I am,

Yours ever,

(signed) Frederick Brown Harris

FOUNDRY METHODIST CHURCH
FREDERICK BROWN HARRIS, D. D.
MINISTER
1500 SIXTEENTH ST. N.W.
WASHINGTON, D.C.

Hon. Marvin McIntyre,
The White House
Washington, D.C.

fdb

Appendix C.

Press Release, July 1, 1943

FOR THE PRESS IMMEDIATE RELEASE JULY 1, 1943

The President has commuted the death sentence of Max Stephan of Detroit to imprisonment for the term of his natural life. The man was properly convicted of treason. He was guilty.

The statute provides the death penalty, or at the discretion of the Court, imprisonment for not less than five years, together with fines. Thus the statute definitely contemplates, with respect to the sentence, treason of different qualities.

In the case of the saboteurs who landed from German submarines—members of the German armed forces but wearing civilian clothes—a mature plan was concocted in Germany, initiated by the men in question and to be carried out in detail in the United States. Their offenses were, therefore, akin to a carefully planned murder in the first degree. Six of them were executed; one received life sentence and one was given thirty years at hard labor.

In the case of Stephan, however, his treason did not come from a plan maturely initiated by him. A German prisoner, who escaped from Canada and was put in touch with Stephan after reaching the city, stated that he was trying to escape in order to rejoin the German armed forces, and was assisted by Stephan in proceeding to the next place. There is no question in the President's mind that Stephan was, and probably is, pro-German or pro-Nazi.

His treason, however, was not part of a preconceived plan. His treason bore something of a parallel to murder in the second degree or manslaughter in the first degree.

Therefore, his case was less of an offense than the case of the saboteurs last year.

The President believes that the sentence imposed by the Court was too severe in that it did not sufficiently take into account the statute which provides for the consideration of different qualities of treason. Stephan will go to prison for life, and the President hopes that no one of his successors will commute that sentence.

Appendix D.

Reaction to Press Release;

1. Letter from V. J. Obenauer, Jr.
2. Letter from Mrs. Kenneth Long
3. Letter from Joseph F. Wright.
4. Letter from Supreme Court Justice Jackson.
5. Editorials and letters to editors,
   a. Courier Journal
   b. Evening Star
   c. Washington Post
   d. New York Times
   e. New York Herald Tribune
6. Letter from Judge O'Brien to McIntyre

Associated Dailies of Florida
HEADQUARTERS OFFICE – P.O. BOX 1740
JACKSONVILLE, FLORIDA
7-2-43

Mr. Marvin McIntyre
Secretary to the President
The White House
Washington, D.C.

Dear. Mr. McIntyre:

I feel it is my duty as a citizen to record my protest against the President's commutation of the death sentence imposed by the court, and upheld by higher courts, against Stephan, the traitor.

I have never encountered unfavorable reaction to a presidential act as spontaneous and unanimous. It is my regretful conclusion that this will do much to weaken civilian and military morale.

Sincerely,

(signed) V. J. Obenauer Jr

519 Madison Avenue,
Rochester, Michigan,
July 2, 1943.

Mr. Stephen Early,
Secretary to President Roosevelt,
The White House,
Washington, D.C.

Dear Sir:

Without a question of doubt you will be beseiged with letters and wires from outraged citizens at the President's interference with the sentence of Max Stephan. I wish to add my vote of strong protest to the others you will receive, and when you hand your tabulation to the President you may wish to know my comments represent the ideas of a great many fellow-workers in the war plant of General Motors Truck and Coach, Pontiac, Michigan, where I am employed.

The President courted the vote of labor when he vetoed the anti-strike bill—is he now courting the vote of the subversive elements in our country by protecting men convicted of treason? It is the bitter regret of many of us that we must wait another year until we are able to vote against the big-time politician we are now forced to accept as our President. What a great day it will be for these United States when we elect a man who puts the interests of the Country before his own petty, personal interests. It becomes more and more apparent there is another other than Hitler who is mad for power.

Such action makes patriotic people who love their country ashamed to call Franklin Roosevelt an American.

Yours very truly,

(signed) Elizabeth Long
Mrs. Kenneth L. Long.

JOSEPH F. WRIGHT
3300 BOOK TOWER, DETROIT
CAdillac 4662

July 2 1943

Dear Mr. President:

Max Stephan lives today, but I'm afraid he's placed another nail in your political coffin. John L Lewis, the "Eleanor Clubs" and your conduct of the domestic economy generally are alienating a great part of the voting public (the solid middle class vote) away from you.

If you don't watch the home front the ground may be cut out from under you on the main objective—winning the war.

Americans love a fight. We're in one now and not 10% of us are fighting mad. Instead of hating the enemy we are beginning to hate those of other groups within our own country.

People don't like to change horses but you can't expect them to keep riding behind one that shies and bolts at every little cloud of dust.

Yours very truly

(signed) Joseph F. Wright

Supreme Court of the United States
Washington, D.C.

CHAMBERS OF
ROBERT H. JACKSON

My dear Mr. President

I am glad and think it both wise and just that you have commutated the death sentence of Max Stephan. In calmer times, whatever the technical merits of the case, the court's sentence will seem savage in proportion to the offense. Thank God man does not distort your own sense of fitness of things.

Faithfully yours
(signed) Robert H. Jackson

To the President
July 2nd 1943

THE POINT OF VIEW

Is it fair to the American people, it is asked, to feed and house for life a man who was a traitor?

The Stephan Clemency

To the Editor of The Courier-Journal.

Several years ago, it was not uncommon at all for any American citizen to read in a daily newspaper that several Americans, French, British or Russians were decapitated by a Nazi executioner after being found guilty by a special military court for conspiring against the Third Reich. Many fell under the blade of the executioner as a result of hasty military trials. This was before the present war. Today what are they doing? Are they bothering to give long trials and hearings to the accused, or, maybe, do the accused die of some illness or another before a trial is held?

It was a strong blow to the American people to hear that the President had commuted the death sentence of Max Stephan to life imprisonment. Is it fair and just to the American people that they have to feed and house for the remainder of his life a man who, by his actions, favored the victory of the German nation over America? Max Stephan was justly convicted by a court and was sentenced to be hanged. Therefore, this should have been carried out.

If this method of dealing with agents of foreign countries is to continue, then how can we expect to rid our country of these people? This method just leads them to believe that if they are caught, the worst that can happen is a few years in prison and then most likely release after the war.

We must serve warning to the Axis nations that their agents' actions in this country will not be tolerated, that they will be given a fair trial and, if found guilty, the death sentence will be executed.

Louisville. WM. R. ALLEN.

Might Give the Boys a Shot

To the Editor of The Courier-Journal.

The commuting of the sentence of Max Stephan the pro-Nazi must, indeed, have been good news to those of the Third Reich and will undoubtedly make a lot of votes over here from among the Bund and its followers, the so-called naturalized ones. Why not send this man back to the Germany he loves so well? Hitler may put him in the army and, perhaps, one of our boys can get a shot at him.

My daddy left that country in the late Fifties and was glad to be rid of it.

Louisville.

GROVER SCHULER.

THE EVENING STAR 7/2/43

Mercy for a Traitor

Max Stephan, convicted traitor, had little reason to hope for mercy at the hands of the Nation he tried to betray.

There is noe evidence whatsoever that he has the slightest sense of loyalty to the United States. Born in Germany, he became a naturalized citizen of this country and accepted all of the benefits that went with his citizenship. But there was no feeling of gratitude in his heart. After he had been convicted of treason for assisting in the escape of a captured Nazi aviator, Stephan said: "My blood is German. I am not sorry for what I have done and I would do it again." In this same period he openly proclaimed his belief in a German victory and boasted that Hitler would never let him hang.

In sentencing Stephan to death, the trial judge made it clear that he was imposing the supreme penalty as a deterrent to other fifth columnists who might also want to give aid and comfort to the enemy.

"We have been too soft, to the extent of being mushy," the judge said. "There are too many in the sob squad and too few in the fighting squad. * * * If the lives of many of our boys are to be taken (in combat), this court should not hesitate to take the life of one traitor" if that, in turn, will help win the war by discouraging other actual or potential traitors.

The logic of this view is persuasive. There is probably nothing that Stephan would not have done to aid his native land in its war against his adopted country. And there is a possibility that this clemency which has been shown him may encourage others to dabble in treason, believing that their lives will not be forfeited if caught.

Granting all of this, however, there is something in the minds of most men which will convince them that the decision the President has made is the right one. The picture that we get of Stephan, weeping and kissing the hands of the lawyer who brought him the news that he had been saved from the gallows, is not a pleasant one. We will win the war, whether Stephan lives or dies, and on the day of victory most of us will be glad that the Government of the United States did not take the life of this thoroughly contemptible individual.

WASHINGTON POST 7/4/43

Max Stephan

Fortunately we are free of much of the war hysteria which disfigured our participation in the last war. But occasionally it crops out. One instance was the death penalty meted out to Max Stephan, the benighted Detroiter who gave assistance to an escaped Nazi prisoner of war who visited Detroit while trying to flee from Canada to his fatherland. Treason, to be sure, is the highest of all crimes. But, as defined in the Constitution, there must be no conviction except where there has been an overt act with at least two witnesses. Stephan, on the contrary, was not party to the escape, nor was he connected with any conspiracy. To be sure, he is an ardent pro-Nazi, with a loyalty to his native land above that to his adopted country, and he did give aid and comfort to a war prisoner. But for what he did in his emotion was done on the spur of the moment, and surely did not merit the same punishment as would be meted out to saboteurs who deliberate as well a commit crimes against our Nation's security.

In the circumstances the President's commutation of the sentence to life imprisonment, with the expressed hope that none of his successors will set it aside, is a punishment befitting Stephan's crime. There are degrees of treason and in this case the crime was certainly not of the first degree. So far as we can gather from the trial, the Detroiter was primarily a fool, and the President is to be complimented on turning his face against a demonstration of war hysteria which would have condemned this fool to the gallows. It took courage to be clement. But those who are zealous to keep our institutions intact while waging the war without mercy will be grateful to the Chief Executive. Perhaps the judges of this country will take note of what the President said. The judge in this case played upon the basest instincts in his charge to the jury. He said, "We have been too soft, to the extent of being mushy. There are too many in the sob squad and too few in the fighting squad. This is no ordinary war. We talk of soldiers and we think of death, not in figures of thousands, but in figures of millions." Such a charge was an affront to the dignity of the bar and reflected discredit on the man who made it.

NEW YORK TIMES 7/3/43

A SENTENCE COMMUTED

The President gives as his reason for commuting the death sentence of Max Stephan his belief that the death penalty imposed by the court in this case "did not sufficiently take into account the statute which provides for the consideration of different qualities of treason." Stephan is the Detroit restaurant-keeper who gave food and lodging to a German flier in his escape from a Canadian prison camp in April of last year. The President says that "the man was properly convicted of treason; he was guilty." But he was guilty, in the President's considered judgment, of a crime which differed from that for which the penalty of execution was imposed on the saboteurs who landed from German submarines, in that his treason "did not come from a plan maturely initiated by him." "His treason bore something of a parallel to murder in the second degree or manslaughter in the first degree."

The law under which Stephan was tried and found guilty specifically provides imprisonment, even for as short a term as five years, as an alternative to the death sentence. Thus the law definitely contemplates, with respect to the sentence; treason or different qualities. The President believes that imprisonment for life, which he has imposed on Stephan as an alternative to the death sentence, is a sufficiently severe penalty for the particular crime involved.

We believe that Americans will find it a sign of our strength, rather than our weakness, that even in wartime the President of the United STates can weigh "the consideration of different qualities of treason" and impose punishment commensurate with the degree and nature of the offense. In this respect our position is in the sharpest possible contrast to the unreasoning and indiscriminating action of our enemies.

NEW YORK HERALD TRIBUNE 7/2/43

The President Is Right

The President's decision in the case of Max Stephan was not an easy one to make, but this newspaper feels that it was right. The man was guilty of treason, and in this day, when so many lives may be taken by a treachery and when our enemies have brought the black arts of treason, espionage, subtle disloyalty and disruption to such great and scientific heights, that is not a crime which can be taken with less than deadly seriousness. There are probably too many others who think their allegiance is a small thing or are convinced, like Stephan, that at any rate "Hitler won't let them hang."

But the President's distinction between degrees of the crime was an appropriate one. Stephan did not act in accordance with a preconceived plan; he seems not to have been part of an organized conspiracy, and to exact from him the same death penalty which was imposed on such deliberate enemies as the Nazi saboteurs would have been excessive. It would have been felt as contrary to American standards of humanity and justice, and might therefore have defeated its purpose. The life sentence should stand as sufficient warning.

PROBATE COURT OF WAYNE COUNTY
DETROIT, MICHIGAN

PATRICK H. O'BRIEN
JUDGE

July 19, 1943

My dear Mr. McIntyre:

I want to thank you for your very prompt and gracious attention to my telephone message in the case of Max Stephan.

You will be glad to know that the decision of the President in commuting the death sentence to life imprisonment was very well received in the metropolitan district of Detroit.

Again thanking you for our cordiality, and with kindest personal regards, I remain

Most sincerely yours,

(signed) Judge Patrick H. O'Brien

Mr. Marvin H. McIntyre
Secretary to the President
The White House
Washington, D.C.

Appendix E.

Miscellaneous:

1. Members of the Supreme Court in early 1943.
2. List of exhibits at trial of Max Stephan.
3. Equivalent Ranks.
4. Maps
    a. Detroit
    b. Krug's Escape Route

The U.S. Supreme Court in Early 1943

Name	Home State	Age	Term Start
Owen J. Roberts	Penn.	68	May 9, 1930
Hugo L. Black	Ala.	57	Aug. 12, 1937
Stanley F. Reed	Ky.	59	Jan. 15, 1938
Felix Frankfurter	Mass.	61	Jan. 15, 1939
William O. Douglas	Conn.	45	Mar. 20, 1939
Frank Murphy	Mich.	50	Jan. 2, 1940
Harlan F. Stone (1)	N.Y.	71	Jun. 12, 1941
Robert H. Jackson	N.Y.	51	Jun. 12, 1941
Wiley B. Rutledge	Iowa	49	Feb. 8, 1943

(1) Chief Justice

List of Exhibits at Trial of Max Stephan

- Naturalization Records
- Epaulets
- Billfold
- Necktie
- Travelling Bag
- Registration card showing Hans Müller registered at Field Hotel
- Greyhound Bus map called "Defense Map of America"
- Mathews Atlas of the World at War
- Scrap of paper chewed by Krug
- Revolver
- Cartridges
- Photo of Krug
- Original statement by Stephan to FBI

Equivalent Commissioned Officer Ranks in the Air Forces of Germany, England, and the U.S.

World War II

Luftwaffe	Royal Air Force	U.S. Army Air Force
Reichsmarschall (1)		
Generalfeldmarschall	Marshall of the RAF	General of the Army
Generaloberst	Air Chief Marshal	General
General der Flieger	Air Marshal	Lieutenant General
Generalleutnant	Air Vice Marshal	Major General
Generalmajor	Air Commodore	Brigadier General
Oberst	Group Captain	Colonel
Oberstleutnant	Wing Commander	Lieutenant Colonel
Major	Squadron Leader	Major
Hauptman	Flight Lieutenant	Captain
Oberleutnant	Flying Officer	First Lieutenant
Leutnant	Pilot Officer	Second Lieutenant

(1) Unique rank held only by Hermann Goering. He ranked above all other officers in the German Armed Forces.

Above information is from *Duel of Eagles* by Peter Townsend.

SCENE OF HANS PETER KRUG ACTIVITIES IN DETROIT

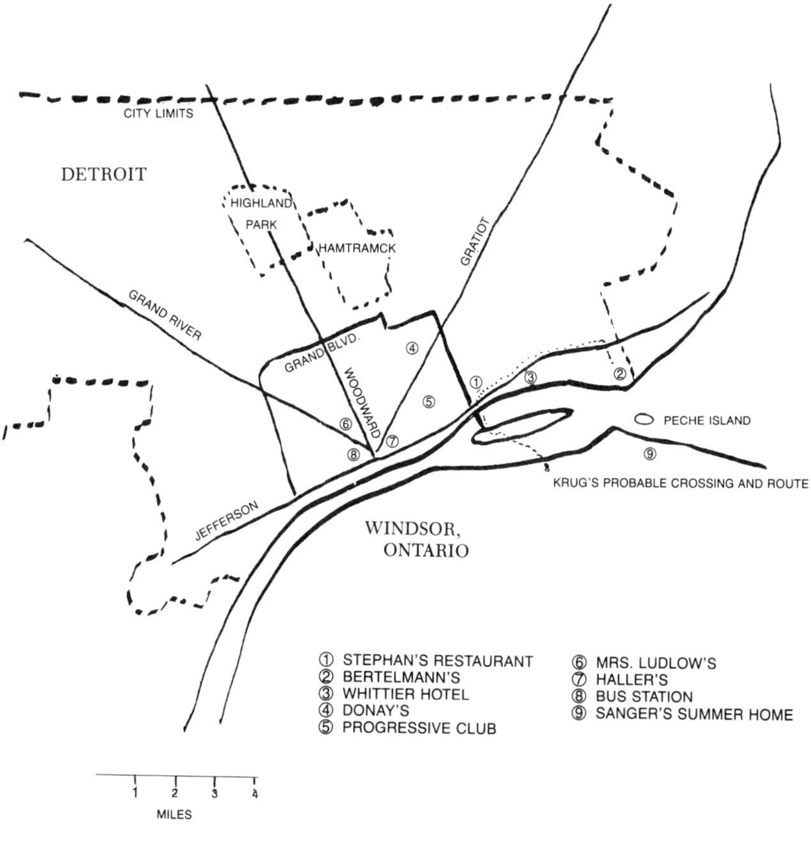

Krug's Escape Route
1942

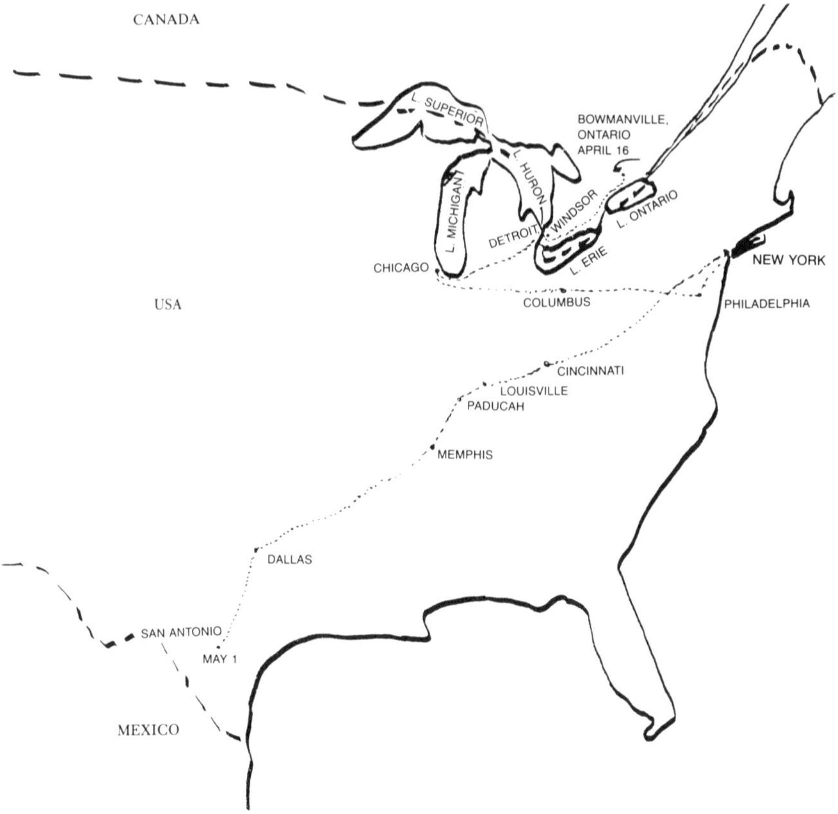

Bibliography

[1]Burt, Kendall; Leasor, James, *The One That Got Away*, Random House, 1956

This is an account of von Werra's escape and of his subsequent return to Germany in April of 1941.

[2]Robertson, Terence, *The Golden Horseshoe*, London, Evans, 1956

[3]Townsend, Peter, *Duel of Eagles*

[4]Zehnder, Herman, *Teach My People the Truth*,

This book describes the history of Frankenmuth, Michigan and contains the account of Judge Tuttle and the punishment he dealt to Fischer and Zehnder. The author is, of course, related to the Zehnder that Tuttle fined so heavily.

[5]Collier, Richard, *Eagle Day*, E.P. Dutton and Co., 1956

[6]Lawson, Ted W., *Thirty Seconds over Tokyo*, Random House, 1943

[7]Melady, John, *Escape From Canada*, McMillan of Canada, 1981

[8]Bergamini, David, *Japan's Imperial Conspiracy*, William Morrow, 1971

I strongly recommend this book to anyone with a serious interest in Japan's role in World War II. It is a book of epic proportions, backed by the most comprehensive of research.

[9]Brown, J.C., *The Case of the Bad Samaritan*, Detroit Magazine—Detroit Free Press, Feb. 15, 1976

[10]Stalmann, R., *Die Ausbrecher Konige von Kanada*, (The Escape Kings of Canada)

This book was originally a series of articles in the German magazine "*Stern*" (Star). The stories were published in book form under the "Escape Kings" name, 1958. In 1973 the book was republished. This book was the major source of details of Peter Krug's escape, from planning to recapture in San Antonio.

[11]Hurst, James Willard, *The Law of Treason in the United Stated*, Greenwood Publishing Corp., 1971

[12]President Roosevelt's "Max Stephan" file, Roosevelt Library, Hyde Park, NY.

[13]Trial transcript of "The United States of America vs. Max Stephan"

[14]FBI Files of Max Stephan case, Washington, DC.

[15]The Detroit Times

[16]The Detroit News

[17]The Detroit Free Press